Captain of
My Soul

Captain of My Soul

MASTERING A DESTINY ALTERED

David Rippy

ISBN: 1537019600
ISBN 13: 9781537019604
Library of Congress Control Number: 2016913283
CreateSpace Independent Publishing Platform
North Charleston, South Carolina

This book is dedicated to my incredible parents. Without their unconditional love and support, my journey would not have been possible.

Table of Contents

Foreword

I WAS ALONE; MY SIDE of the car and roof were caved in around me. Blood was starting to trickle down my face slowly, and I couldn't wipe it away, no matter how hard I struggled. My arms and legs wouldn't move. I estimated about a half hour had gone by since my friend had left to get help. Thankfully, he wasn't seriously injured. His side of the car had considerable damage, but with great effort, he managed to get the door unjammed. As he crawled up the steep, slippery embankment through the dark woods to the empty roadside above, I was glad I had thought to ask him to drape his coat over me before he left. My window and half of the windshield were now gone, bringing in the frigid outside air. It was a light jacket, not nearly adequate for my injury on this late October night, but somehow it seemed to help, I wasn't shivering as much now.

The road was covered with a thick blanket of fog; it would be a miracle at this time of night if his frantic gestures for help drew any response. Adding to the difficulty, cell phones and GPS were not yet widely available commercially, and neither of us was familiar with this desolate stretch of highway. I seemed to have pieces of glass embedded in my face, but fortunately, they were not in my eyes. I could still see out of both of them, thank God. At that moment, though, I couldn't see much of anything; the dim glow from the lights of the dash had faded away. The battery had finally succumbed to the accident, much like the car engine earlier. I wasn't sure if I was entering shock from what I thought was a broken neck, or the growing bloodstain soaking through one of my gray pant legs. Both my knees remained jammed against the dash, and I couldn't free them to check. I was exhausted; it had already been a long day, which was turning into a much longer night.

I closed my eyes, no longer finding a reason to keep them open. I thought if I kept them shut, it would hopefully keep the blood from blinding me. The situation I now found myself in was something you would want to block out. To look down at my still and slumped body, now unable to move anything, was not a sight I cared to see.

Introduction

"Being challenged in life is inevitable, being defeated is optional."

–Roger Crawford

As I sit now, I am in a wheelchair, paralyzed from the shoulders down. I was in the prime of my life when my world changed forever: athletic, six months out of college and just starting a new position offering a potentially rewarding career path with a Fortune 50 company. Initially, my survival was dependent on the doctors and the medical procedures I underwent. Later, my journey and successes were dictated mainly by the powers of my mind and consciousness, something we are all capable of doing. This is not to say I have not experienced a few medical setbacks along the way, requiring conventional modalities. It simply means that I have made an effort to discover and learn more about myself, who "I AM," and in the process, gained valuable insights and knowledge that helped lead to greater realizations from the tough challenges and setbacks I faced.

In the immediate days, weeks, and months following my accident, I could not have known where this journey would take me. I found that prayer and meditation made it easier to continue forward, though I didn't actively pursue meditation until years after my accident. While spirituality is an abstract concept, one that has no confines or boundaries, we do not require an intermediary or third party to interpret our personal message for us. It is as simple as looking inside, and anyone can seek what I have found. In my earlier years, living with the aftermath of the accident and resultant paralysis, I decided to reach down deep into the core of my character to discover more about myself and what was possible. I was also fortunate, compared to many, in that I had a strong support staff, a loving family, and friends to help me through. My path, though difficult, is less dark and the way forward, less challenging than what others may face because of my blessings.

After the prognosis from a team of top-flight neurosurgeons who deemed my paralysis from the shoulders down permanent, I realized I had a long and uncertain journey ahead. As the road stretched out before me, I knew that the chapters of my life were yet to be written, and it was up to me to decide how I would fill the pages. While the pages could have been scribed with an underlying tone of self-pity, marked by a defeatist attitude—that is not the path I chose. Instead, I decided to recount a life of trials, lessons, and experiences, where defeats and setbacks could have a positive outcome as well. Even our smallest victories or greatest hardships in life propel us forward to greater understanding of not only ourselves, but of others and their lives. To some reading this disappointed perhaps with not discovering a journey marked by tremendous wealth, celebrity or the highest of social status, maybe the lens we are viewing through is somewhat different. I assure you, my journey will lead us to common ground.

The pages in this book are my reflections, recollections, confessions, my hopes and my dreams. Mere words seem almost inadequate when I try to convey all that I have seen and been through, but words are all I have. It is my sincerest hope and wish that my story might bring some comfort, insights, and greater understanding into the journey of others who have shouldered heavy burdens. Hopefully along the way, gaining a stronger vision of who they are as unique individuals and what is possible. I have faith that God is not done with me yet, that I have more to accomplish, and that He will be guiding and supporting me along the way.

As William Ernest Henley wrote in his poem, *"Invictus,"*

It matters not how strait the gate,

How charged with punishment the scroll,

I am the master of my fate,

I am the captain of my soul.

This is the story of my life and my miracles.

Weekend of the Accident

~

"Life has many ways of testing a person's will, either by having nothing happen at all, or by having everything happen all at once."

−Paulo Coelho

I HAD ONLY BEEN HOME three weeks since moving from Texas, having just accepted a new position with a large Fortune 50 company six months upon graduating. My parents were still living in the same two-story house where I had spent the last two years of high school and my college years. The house was situated on a cul-de-sac in a nice suburban neighborhood; it was a wonderful place to return to after being gone for several years and presented a nice chance to catch up with the family.

My folks were happy. Another of their offspring had graduated college and landed a job, one that appeared to have a bright future. Their three oldest had now graduated from different colleges and were applying for job positions or had already started careers. Another brother was a sophomore in college, and their youngest son was finishing high school and attending college the following September. My parents' respective careers were also going well. Things couldn't have looked brighter.

There was a sense of optimism I carried in with me each morning to my new position. I would arrive around eight am to meet Bob who was training me as his replacement. Bob was happy to do the training; he was retiring after forty years with the company and was ready to relax and enjoy more time on the various golf courses in the area. I was fortunate to have the opportunity and Bob, with his many years of experience, was a sharp and good-natured person to teach me the ropes.

The position involved the complete management of two immense industrial corporate centers with multi-national clients as tenants. The clients ranged from McDonald's, with their massive distribution plant at one of our locations, to Ferrari of North America. Ferrari would ship straight out of their manufacturing facility in Italy to one of these industrial parks for distribution to their dealerships east of the Mississippi. I went to their office to introduce myself to management and then toured their huge warehouse where rows and rows of gleaming red and black Ferraris were lined up. I watched while high-end mechanics and detailers performed the final tests, applying the last coats of high gloss wax before shipping to dealers around the country. I was tasked with managing approximately 150 tenants at these two vast locations on everything from warehouse conditions, utilities, to *101 different possibilities*, according to Bob. The position also involved hiring various contractors for maintenance issues, collecting and reconciling monthly rents, utility bills, as well as all expenses associated with these clients. By week's end, I looked forward to relaxing—listening to music, enjoying a few beers out with friends and unwinding at one of the local clubs nearby.

Another day in the office

Saturday night was like any typical Saturday night: an evening at a local nightspot, dancing and having fun. I decided to hit a new club with a friend that boasted a large dance floor, a state of the art sound system and was known for playing top dance music. They even had a robot that would go out on stage, dancing and mingling with the patrons. The friend who was accompanying me I had met at a local moving company where I had worked several summers between college semesters. I hadn't been to this club since Christmas break ten months earlier and when we arrived there was quite a crowd already on the floor, dancing to a top club hit. I ordered a beer at the bar and asked a girl to dance. The music was upbeat, and the DJ was keeping the energy high throughout the evening. After a fun-filled night and dancing until closing, my friend and I made our way through the parking lot to his car. It was about 2:15 in the morning. As we were getting in the car, I noticed three girls outside of their car obviously having trouble getting inside. I yelled over to see if they needed help and one remarked that they had locked their keys in. I walked over and tried the doors first, finding they were all locked, but noticed that one of the windows was cracked about an inch. Fortunately, they had an inside door lock that resembled a golf tee, providing an opportunity to gain entry, if we could locate a wire coat hanger. My friend ran back to the club and retrieved one from the coatroom. I had been locked out of my car a few times and had become somewhat adept at gaining entry to mine. By straightening out a coat hanger and using one open end to fashion a hook-like device, with some bending, one could hopefully catch the door lock plunger to gain access.

After about twenty minutes of maneuvering, the door lock finally sprang free. The girls thanked us and quickly got in their car, started the motor and made their way out of the parking lot. As I glanced around, ice crystals were forming on all the cars. I was glad to be inside my friend's vehicle; the temperature was dropping outside, and I was looking forward to the heater warming up. The highway was practically empty, and being one way, we exited right, making our way to the next light to turn around and head in the direction of home. Generally, during the morning through early evening, this major North–South U.S. Highway serves a large portion of the east coast of the United States and is extremely busy. You would never have known that now, it was silent and desolate at about 2:45 am, with only the occasional car or truck.

There was a noticeable fog starting to roll in, though not enough to impair vision to a great extent. As my friend drove, the fog became noticeably thicker, starting to obscure the roads surface, and was now up to three or four feet high. It was easy enough to discern other vehicles on the road from their lights, and I could still see the guardrails on the side. As the highway dipped, the fog was unusually thick, our headlights barely penetrating. Suddenly, we were not on the road anymore. The car must've hit something—I had no idea what and the vehicle was no longer moving. I was dazed, had slid forward in my seat, and the only visibility was from the dim glow emanating from the dashboard lights. The car was dead, tilted at about a thirty-degree angle. After a few moments, I still had no idea what had just occurred; everything had happened so quickly.

My friend was equally dazed and was starting to stir. As he slowly moved around groaning in pain, he wiped the blood off his face. It appeared he had hit his head on the rearview mirror of his car. It was no longer attached to the windshield and must have ripped off in the process. I tried to straighten myself back up in my seat, but there was a noticeable disconnect between my mental efforts and my body. A shocking revelation sank in as I struggled unsuccessfully to right myself. I found I couldn't move my arms or legs. I kept trying, but I remained motionless, wedged down inside this little car. I felt panic creep in, an emotion that I had little familiarity with until now. The inability to move my arms or legs was unnerving, and I couldn't help but feel a wave of helplessness begin to sweep over me. The extent of my injury was becoming shockingly apparent to me.

My first instinct was to try and think through my predicament and just push aside any thoughts of the accident or my injury. But I was dealing with what seemed like a surreal, slow motion nightmare, one that I could not wake from, made even more apparent by my futile attempts. There wasn't enough visibility to see much and I couldn't even move my head, limited now to just staring straight ahead. Time didn't have any purpose in those moments, basically non-existent, just standing still as the enormity of the event started to overwhelm me.

I worked hard to snap myself back mentally from the horrific thoughts that blazed throughout my mind, engulfing everything in its path. Somehow and someway, I found a stable, more logical and calm place within and it helped bring me back, if only long enough to try and figure something out. I realized loud and clear that time was precious and did have relevance; every minute trapped in these dark, cold woods could mean making it…or *that's it.*

I asked my friend if he could try to pry open his door and get help. After considerable effort and struggle, he managed to dislodge his door, only wide enough to squeeze out. Thankfully his door's locking mechanism wasn't jammed, though the door was crumpled and the hinges now limited to the most minor of movement. He painfully crawled out into the darkness, slipping on the wet and steep bank. The car was now wedged amongst trees on an embankment, way off the road in dense and unfamiliar woods. I called him over and after considerable effort holding onto the crumpled car for support, he was able to make it around to my side of the car. I then in what seemed a surprisingly calm, almost disembodied voice, sounding so measured in light of what I was experiencing let him know the seriousness of my injury. Very direct and to the point, I shared, *"I'm all messed up, I think my neck is broken, and you have to go alone and find help."* I'm not sure what was registering in his mind with that statement. I could no longer turn my head to see the look on his face, as I was now forced to just stare straight ahead. He was quiet, just standing in the dark at my side of the car.

The blown out windows and mangled roof on my side of the car were bringing in the frigid air, and I was starting to shiver. I could see my breath so I asked him to lay his coat on me before he left. I vaguely recalled something about shock possibly setting in from serious injury and blood loss. Perhaps they were memories from an old Boy Scout first aid class, a movie, or just some parental lessons that were filtering back into my consciousness. Who knows? I just knew that I wasn't dressed appropriately to survive long in this cold and considering the physical state I was in, was hoping my friend could make it to the roadside above, let alone find some help. Without the barrier of the dash of his car, I also realized I would have just slid down in a crumpled heap on the car floor if there were enough room to afford such a maneuver. Thankfully, there wasn't.

Following the car's downward trajectory backward up the hill, my friend made his way gingerly up the slippery grade. The plan was to try and flag someone down, no easy task. It was approximately 3:00 in the morning on a foggy highway without a car in sight. The possibility he would be successful was remote, if not highly improbable. But he had to be successful; I was trapped in these dark woods alone now and time was precious. Blood was starting to trickle down my face, and I couldn't wipe it off. I speculated it was the result of the glass flying in from the shattered and blown out windows from the car's contact with the trees, or my head may have grazed the collapsed roof.

I estimated about a half hour had gone by since my friend had left to get help, I couldn't lift my arm to check my watch, and the car's radio clock was frozen at the time we hit the trees. Slumped there alone in the dark, cold and bleeding, the embedded glass, fortunately, didn't seem to be near my eyes. I could still see out of both of them, thank God. The lights of the dash had already faded, having served initially to add a dim glow in the cockpit of the car. The battery had finally succumbed to the accident, much like the car engine earlier. I was exhausted, unsure if I was entering shock from my neck injury or blood loss, most likely from both. I couldn't bend my head down to see, and could only lower my eyes to the bottom of their sockets. I had noticed a great, ominous bloodstain seeping through my right pant leg near my knee before the remaining light faded.

It was pitch black, and I couldn't tell if my knee was still bleeding, though I thought it was. I closed my eyes, no longer finding a reason to keep them open. Also with them closed, I reasoned, I could hopefully keep the blood that was coming down my face from blinding me.

I must have passed out. I don't remember anything after I closed my eyes. I came to as they wheeled my stretcher through what I thought was a hospital's emergency room. The early morning shift of doctors and trauma nurses were rushing me down a corridor. I glanced up, the only thing I could do, watching the fluorescent lights in the ceiling pass above me quickly, brightly lit rectangles starting to blur together as their pace quickened.

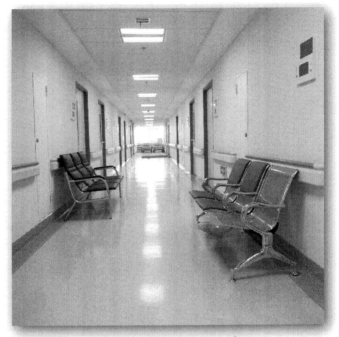

Hospital emergency corridor

They eventually stopped the stretcher, and I began to tell them I could not move my body, that I thought my neck was broken. The doctors paid little heed, more focused on my bleeding and blood-soaked right pant leg. They cut the pants off quickly, and the doctors started to clean the area. The cleaning revealed deep, wide gashes on and around my right knee, serious lacerations from my knees' impact with the dashboard. When their coagulants finally succeeded in halting the blood flow, they started moving my stretcher to X-ray. A short time later, the X-rays would show a hairline fracture of the patella in my right knee, presenting images of what your kneecap would look like if you smashed a trashcan lid flat. They were now starting to hear my clearly voiced concerns involving my neck. After a few preliminary pinprick pain tests, coupled with some medical staff requests to move this or that, the doctors were now getting the picture I tried to paint an hour earlier. I knew my bleeding knee had to be their first concern; bleeding out would have made my neck injury moot.

My parents arrived around five in the morning after being contacted by the hospital. I had never witnessed them this upset before. One of their children was severely injured, and there was nothing they could do. Years later, my sister told me that it was the only time she had ever seen our father cry.   My care would be up to the abilities of this hospital's trauma center staff and what they could accomplish. My life was literally in their hands at this point.

As I lay there and the ER staff continued working on me, I never considered that a night out with a friend, dancing and having fun, would find me roughly two hours after leaving the club in an emergency trauma center. They ordered x-rays of my neck region, and when they came back, they revealed I had two broken vertebrae, cervical four and five, with my spinal cord pinched in-between. There were broken vertebrae fragments scattered throughout the damaged cord in the region. Stabilization of my neck was becoming the priority as the surgeon finished stitching my knee back together.

The trauma nurses, working together, immobilized my knee and leg in an inflatable cast, as the doctors discussed and reviewed the X-rays of my neck. After consulting my parents, the doctors decided that the best course of action was to stretch the vertebrae in my neck apart, hoping that it would help to free the damaged cord. It would also allow the neurosurgeons a less obstructed X-ray view of the spinal cord and a greater ability to assess the magnitude of the damage. This procedure would also help the surgeons determine the best surgical possibilities to stabilize for the long-term. As I listened to the various doctors exchange thoughts between themselves, an emergency room nurse came back into the room, carrying large, stainless steel tongs with sharp pointed ends, in her hands. The nurse gave them to a doctor who began positioning them above my head. All I could do was cringe.

I asked the doctor holding the tongs what they planned to do with those, and he replied, "*These are Crutchfield tongs and will be used to stabilize your neck and head region. We want to minimize further damage to your spinal cord."*

With that, a doctor and nurse placed the sharp points about two inches above each of my ears and started turning the lever, tightening the screw as the points began moving closer together in the process. They continued to turn until the sharp ends penetrated through the skin above my ears and on into my skull. I couldn't help but hear the crunching of bone. The pain was intense; my head felt as if it was in a vise with two sharp points now firmly jammed into my skull. The staff checked their work, satisfied that the sharp tong ends were well planted into the bone and wouldn't dislodge. Next, a steel wire was attached on the end of the Crutchfield tongs and then threaded through a pulley on a metal post attached to my stretcher. At the end of the wire, a metal plate was attached, swinging slightly about a foot off the floor. When everything was lined up to their satisfaction, one doctor put his hand on my shoulder and leaning over said, *"Here goes."*

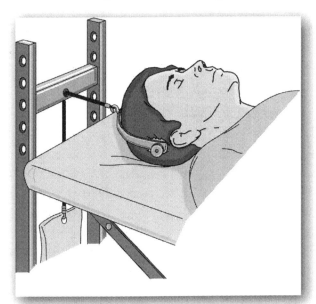

A depiction of Crutchfield Tongs, and stretching of the neck through the use of a pulley and weights.

They began adding ten-pound steel weights, one at a time, very carefully on the empty metal plate. The plan was to stretch my neck far enough to free my damaged spinal cord caught in the crushed vertebrae's grip. I was fully conscious; all I could do was grimace and squint my eyes. Every weight they slowly placed on top of the last stretched my neck a little further, increasing my level of agony to new heights.

The doctors were well aware of my extreme discomfort, noticing that after several ten-pound plates, my cord would not free easily. My neck and shoulders were strong from years of wrestling, weights, and other sports, making the muscles in the region quite contracted. In the process, my neck injury had naturally pulled my shoulders and Trapezius muscles up, contributing to making it even more difficult to X-ray the region. They knew my neck and shoulder muscles had responded in this fashion due to the body's natural defense mechanisms, to help shield damaged areas from additional trauma if possible. The crushed vertebrae were not helping matters either.

Continuing to add ten-pound plates slowly, the surgeons would take measurements after each one and then order another round of X-rays. With eighty pounds now positioned on the metal plate, the Crutchfield tongs, anchored firmly in my skull, the latest set of X-rays showed my spinal cord was still trapped. My neck was on fire. My spinal cord caught, its frayed and damaged nerves shooting excruciating pain signals into my brain with each plate added, an already traumatized area further stressed by this procedure. It was as if a thousand hot needles, fired with electricity, were jammed into my neck while my head was slowly being pulled off my shoulders at the same time. Moans escaped my lips as they slowly added twenty more pounds. Then more X-rays were ordered. The doctors confided they never had to use this much weight before to straighten a neck injury. That was one record I didn't care to have, and I didn't answer, just continuing to grit my teeth and squint my eyes.

Extremely disappointing was that the new X-rays revealed, that even with a hundred pounds of weight hanging off that wire, my cord was still trapped. I had now reached even higher levels of pain, thresholds I had never before experienced. Images of medieval torture devices like the rack came to my mind, where captors would pull limbs off others by increasing the tension until the body could take the strain no longer, and dismemberment would result.

The process of adding plates started again. I now found myself yelling out angrily, *"That's good!"* and *"That's enough weights!"* I had no idea if my spinal cord was free but I had reached my limit and threw in a few choice words to emphasize my point. For a moment, the adding of additional weights had stopped. It was time for more X-rays to see how much had been accomplished due to the additional poundage. I took this opportunity to try to get someone's attention. I knew I wanted to be let in on where this was going from here, to at least have an idea of what to expect as far as my future care. I was tired of being hurt, helpful or not. I didn't expect the doctors to provide lengthy medical jargon of what they had in mind, just simply letting me know in layman's terms what procedures were coming next.

The Crutchfield tongs, their sharp points planted firmly in my head, coupled with the heavy weight now stretching my neck to lengths and limits I didn't think were realistic or humanly possible, had caught me off guard. I was still operating in a survival mindset, the whole situation still feeling very surreal. Though the pain was mind numbing in my neck and head, it was almost as if I was partially removed from the macabre procedures as my sense of feeling was different now below that region. My sensory function was not as intense or noticeable now below my shoulders and chest, contributing to the strangeness of the moment. It had only been a few hours since the accident, and everything taking place from the crash until now was so removed from my normal world, placing me in a semi-shocked state. It was as if I was viewing my life through a well-worn lens at the end of an old periscope. A periscope attached to an equally aged submarine rocking violently in dark and angry seas, locked onto a still body engulfed in bright lights. As I viewed, I heard monitors and alarms going off, as knowledgeable staff swarmed around me wearing blue gloves. The horrific pain helped snap me back a little, as I resolved silently to myself to try and stay as sharp as possible. Hopefully, to gain an understanding of what the doctors had in store, and mentally steel myself for whatever came next.

I wasn't used to not being in control of my situation and unbeknownst to me at the time, my ability to be physically independent again was forever curtailed. Had that knowledge been apparent to me at the time, it would have been enough to make me, and most others I assume, consider whether getting out of those woods alive was worthwhile. Thankfully, soon enough, I realized it was.

I never had painkillers before, nor were they even offered by the medical staff. I didn't ask for any, hadn't even thought about it; everything was happening so fast. I didn't know if they even would have been administered if I had requested, considering my injury. I wasn't being consulted or informed of the procedures as they continued, so I wanted to remain clearheaded if I could. I knew my parents "were in the loop," thankfully, and though my mother was a registered nurse, dealing with acute spinal cord injuries was not her area of expertise. This small hospital's trauma center didn't seem to be that familiar with dealing with traumatic injuries like mine either.

I knew virtually nothing concerning cervical injuries, and I was beginning to wonder if this procedure would eventually stretch my neck out so far it would remain so. The weight adding began anew. As additional plates were carefully added, I yelled out, *"Hey, my neck is killing me from the stretching! What are you trying to do, make me a giraffe!? Can you hear me?!"* I was infuriated and could only feel the blinding pain and an inability to do anything about it wasn't helping. I don't remember them acknowledging my remarks; they seemed to be more engrossed with measuring the additional increases in neck length with each new plate added. Then more notes would be written on their clipboard and new X-rays ordered. When the last X-ray showed the cord no longer caught between the vertebrae, the weight adding stopped and they said that was the end.

The latest X-rays revealed that my spinal cord was free, but there was extensive damage, bone fragments throughout and swelling. They informed me that the fragments couldn't be removed, or the spinal cord stabilized until surgery. There was now one hundred and thirty pounds of weight hanging on that wire.

They went on to tell me even though the cord was now free, the weights would have to be left in place, and that the incredible tension placed on my neck would help alleviate more damage to the splintered vertebrae or spinal cord. As I lay there, listening to this latest revelation, I didn't feel much of anything besides pain, which seemed to have leveled off somewhat, though at a mind-blowing level. Whether it was from the knowledge that there were no more weights to be added or the fact I was so mentally depleted from what seemed like excruciating torture and was now getting a break from it.

Whatever the cause, I find it amazing I didn't pass out during the entire experience. It wasn't like I was some trained secret agent or Buddhist monk, able to separate myself mentally and endure the extreme amount of pain under the most tortuous of circumstances. As mentioned, no sports injury, or anything for that matter, ever came close to what I had just experienced. I was still wide-awake and amazingly clear-headed. I figured that what I would be forced to experience wasn't over by any stretch, or that my mental faculty would be as sharp later as I felt it was now. I was still operating in survival mode, and my body was flooding itself with natural pain-killing endorphins and adrenalin. Both natural defense mechanisms that we all possess which can help alleviate extreme suffering or pain as many have experienced.

I learned early on after several attempts to get more information; the doctors still wanted to share as little as possible. Their responses seemed to be more geared toward just pacifying me. I wasn't sure if that was because this was new territory for them, handling complex trauma cases like mine, or they just didn't have much to share. They were more focused on stabilizing my condition. It was apparent that they cared and were doing all that was possible, considering the limitations they were working under, not being a medical facility that specialized in broken necks or extreme and traumatic patient situations. Later, my mother learned from an orthopedic surgeon friend early on after the accident; it was imperative that I get out of there quickly if possible to a facility that specialized in spinal cord injuries.

There wasn't much they could say; it had only been four hours since I was pulled out of the car. In hindsight, it's possible the doctors weren't even sure I would live much longer. Their silence and lack of information-sharing probably should have spoken volumes to me. I was only twenty-five though and didn't think I was even close to death. I felt trapped in a riveting hospital drama with a horrific plot, one in which I found myself caught in the middle. Fortunately, at least so far, it wasn't something like; *everything that was possible was attempted, but the severity of the injury and extreme trauma to the patient's spinal cord were proving to be too much. His heart and organs were now failing from the shock and strain. The doctors continued working vigilantly to the point of exhaustion, but their efforts were to no avail, this young man was gone.*

As the night continued to unfold, I didn't want to fall asleep or be incognizant of what was taking place. Besides the pain, I knew that physically I was in bad shape, being unable to move anything but my eyes and mouth. Now that my neck was immobilized to their satisfaction, the doctors and nurses began to recheck my body straps. These straps had kept my body still throughout the whole process. Though I couldn't move voluntarily, my body was strong enough to spasm involuntarily and was something that easily could have occurred from all the stress my body was experiencing, possibly causing even more damage to my spinal cord. The medical team re-checked the two-inch-wide leather straps from my ankles to my shoulders, pulling them tighter until the doctors and nurses felt comfortable they were all very taut and secure. They then placed one across my forehead and pulled tight till I could feel the stiff leather starting to make my forehead sore.

As I lay there in pain, my neck stretched to its limits, and my entire body bound I wondered to myself, *did the amazing escape artist and great magician, Houdini, ever think of something like this when coming up with his tortuous escape acts for the stage?* Unlike him, I felt deep in my heart with mounting fear, that I would not be escaping this anytime soon.

The device I was strapped on is called a "Stryker frame," which is a very narrow stretcher with leather straps. Several doctors and nurses drifted in, checked on me, took notes, and drifted out again. They came back in the room after I had been staring at the ceiling for what seemed an eternity, wondering to myself, how could a fun evening out have ended like this, dancing earlier that night and now I can't move? I was now realizing for the first time in my life, how easy it was to take for granted what gifts and opportunities one has without physical limitations. Though these memories are as fresh in my mind now as yesterday and always will be, the sheer, new reality of my changed world wouldn't become fully apparent until days, weeks, months and even years later. Only five hours in, it felt like a nightmare where I was fully awake but couldn't shake myself out.

The doctors and nurses who were assigned to my care crowded around my Stryker frame and one doctor, seemingly in charge, began to tell me the frame had to be rotated 180 degrees every two hours to relieve pressure on my skin and body, to help avoid skin breakdown. Another doctor went to the head of the Stryker and held the tongs planted in my head trying to keep them steady as well as he could. Being that I am a relatively large guy, they had several nurses and hospital aides assist in the rotating of the frame after unlocking its position.

They asked if I was ready to be flipped. Since I had never been flipped before, I didn't know what to expect, but had a strong feeling rotating upside down would most likely hurt like hell. I closed my eyes and tried to brace myself as they began the rotation. As they turned the table, my pain increased to new levels, shooting throughout my neck, as the rotation was in process. After that first flip, I knew I would not be looking forward to the next ones. I was now hanging upside down under the stretcher, my entire body suspended by straps alone, and I was facing a hard surface below me. I imagined what would happen if the straps gave way and I fell on the hard linoleum floor below me, being unable to break my fall.

Though I didn't say anything, one of the nurses must have sensed my trepidation and commented, "the frame is to be turned every two hours, going from facing the ceiling to facing the floor. The straps will keep you secure."

They began to leave again, and I asked if they could turn the lights down. They set them lower while they filed out to see other patients. As I hung there alone, under the Stryker frame in the dimly lit room, I thought about my current predicament. I had not yet fully accepted my situation as permanent. It was still way too early to assess, based on initial surgeon evaluations. It felt permanent to me. I didn't have that tingly feeling one sometimes gets playing sports, which is pretty standard in football and wrestling. The kind of sensation one sometimes feels after being tackled, where your neck bends at an uncomfortable angle or your body is twisted from multiple impacts. Once in a while that feeling would set in accompanied by pain and numbing sensations, shooting through your hands, arms or legs. People who play sports or did, I'm sure can relate to this. As I had played various sports for many years, I had experienced that *pins and needles* feeling in different parts of my body several times. I didn't have those sensations now, not a lot of that feeling below my shoulders, and that made me even more concerned. I blocked those fears in my mind until the doctors made their final assessment, hoping my gut would be wrong, and my life could return to normal.

Hanging upside down, I found myself starting to look at the linoleum tile beneath me. I tried to relax and not let my mind dwell on my situation or the accident. The last twenty-four hours since getting up Saturday morning, the night out, the car crash, getting pulled from the car, and on to the various painful procedures, had left me drained. Now, strangely enough, I was enjoying the solitude, dim room, and silence that for the first time, was mine. I took the opportunity to try and distract my thoughts away from my wretched predicament. As my eyes explored the floor beneath me, I came to realize the linoleum floor under this contraption could have used a little more love from the cleaning staff!

Amazingly, this was a reprieve, if only for a short time. As my eyes checked out the floor underneath me, immobile and suspended, it was the only visual available. I had never actually gazed for a period of time at a floor before, never cared to and wasn't into different types of tile, floors or carpet for that matter, before the accident. Here I was, finding it a welcome distraction, a new experience, albeit an unexciting one, nonetheless, that's all there was and served the purpose. I was just thankful that no insects, or mice for that matter, ran under it. That was a small thing, the dirty floor underneath. The real heavy lifting was coming in roughly another hour and a half, my time to be rotated again. I would have to deal once more with the pain and additional strain placed on my damaged spinal cord and the broken vertebra. The turning of the Stryker frame and the tension on my neck from the weights would remain in place much longer than I could have ever imagined. It would continue over the next three days, rotating that frame twelve times a day, every two hours, over and over.

Though the floor was a slight distraction, I found myself naturally being pulled back mentally to the biggest challenge of my life. As I lay there strapped, turned like a very slow rotisserie chicken, I had every right and inclination to be more upset ... but I wasn't. At this stage, no one knew the extent of my injury, the doctors, my family or me. I hadn't yet had surgery and the doctors could not assess whether the spinal cord injury was permanent. My body was still too traumatized. It could take many months for damaged nerves to heal, if ever. I tried to stay upbeat, due to the unknowns. Only with the passage of time do the unknowns become more apparent.

After roughly three days in this smaller hospital, an opening became available in a large regional teaching hospital specializing in acute spinal cord injuries. Their survival rates were not only higher, but their hospital specialists would ensure that everything possible would be undertaken. Thankfully, my mother, being a nurse for ten years, had been able to discuss my situation with some surgeons at the hospital where she currently worked as a nurse.

One doctor, in particular, told my mother emphatically that I had to get to this Regional Spinal Cord Center without delay, that my chances of survival where I currently was were probably less than 50% when probed. He then provided to my mother's attentive ears, *"and that would be very optimistic."* With his help, arrangements were made for the transfer to the new hospital. Thankfully, he knew my mother and understood the risks of remaining where I was. I owe him an enormous debt; he made a significant contribution on my behalf and was one of several early on, that enabled me to share my story.

Post Surgery

"Once you choose HOPE anything's possible."

—*Christopher Reeves*

My hospital exposure before this accident was very limited, mostly due to sports, goofing off with friends, and taking unnecessary risks on rare occasions through dares and childhood bets. These incidents occasionally led to stitches, a pulled muscle or two, and several times, a severe sprain. Not a whole lot of hospital experience beyond taking my first breath and having my tonsils out at three. Early on, understandable thoughts drifted in my mind, *what if the surgery didn't result in a positive outcome giving me back my mobility?* Practically no sleep marked my days and nights. The surgery had gone well, according to the surgeons. They had fused my fourth and fifth vertebrae together with a wire wrapping and had removed the bone fragments. Next, a stainless steel halo ring was anchored tightly around my head, held firmly in place by four quarter-inch screws, penetrating into my skull.

"The halo ring, with its rigid structure, will keep your head and neck still, providing the necessary time to heal," the neurosurgeon shared, as he checked the screws, torqueing a few in the process deeper into the bone. The doctors then connected the ring to steel bars, which were further attached to a restrictive hard plastic vest, encasing my entire upper body. Lined with warm and irritating fleece, I would have to endure this for the next three months.

Going into my second week since the accident, I was still unable to move a muscle beyond my blinking eyes and mouth. My body was wasting away—a physique I took pride in, having built it up to handle the rigors of various sports and athletic pursuits I enjoyed. I felt more than miserable. The ring holding my head and neck rigid, coupled with the screws anchored tightly in my skull, was extremely uncomfortable and painful. I was completely immobile, my mind racing, as my eyes continually scanned the new little hospital room. The room didn't offer a heck of a lot for my mind to process. The monitors were positioned almost out of my eyesight; the glow from their illuminated fronts sharing my vital statistics was barely catching the far corner of my left eye. As I strained my eyes to the right, there wasn't much to reveal there either. I could only view the top of the door on that side and hear busy activity up and down the halls when the monitors weren't setting off one of the multiple alarms, alarms in machines tethered to electrodes on my body and IVs in my veins. Then a flash of humanity usually garbed in white would streak around me, shutting off the alarm, usually sharing that things were "fine," and streak out the door again. The wall across from me was blank, nothing but a drab coat of white paint.

A few days later, my sister thoughtfully brought in an oversized print of a mountain scene, originally painted by Albert Bierstadt, to hang on the wall. He was best known for his large, panoramic paintings of the American West. The picture was complete with a stream and several deer eating foliage in front of a sweeping, mountainous backdrop. How ironic; a gathering of deer in the painting and it was a large dead deer in our lane that caused my friend's car to careen off the road that night. It would later be determined that another driver had struck it before we arrived, its sad and possibly still dying body lying there while we struck it again. Pennsylvania has the dubious distinction of being among the top three states in the nation, in which deer are hit by automobiles and trucks over a ten-year average. No signage posted anywhere near this stretch warned of that possibility. The deer in the picture never bothered me, and it did provide some life and beauty to the empty wall, which was what my *dear* sister had in mind. In her haste and concern, she didn't even notice they were there. She was just trying to bring in something to help brighten my rough situation and spruce up an empty and sterile wall.

Most times of the day or night, lying there in my room, a stream of voices would fly by my semi-open door, and the activity would cast intermittent light into my room. Unable to see the source outside my door due to my restrained visibility, I would notice the sounds first, preceded by the broken light emanating in from the hall. Once in a while, telltale squeaks would filter into my room followed in turn by a longer shadow, from what I knew was the occasional stretcher as it rolled by. The nurses cast mostly quick shadows as they flew by with their light footsteps, off to another patient's room. Then the fluorescent light outside of my room would return uninterrupted for a time.

Sometimes I caught small bursts of broken conversations, mostly the staff's busy talk amongst each other, as they shared notes and any new information on their patients. Usually, their exchanges came in under their breath as they congregated in the hall near my room. I never was sure if it was me or the patient next door they were discussing. As the monitors beeped away, I strained my ears intently, to pick up whatever was said. Was it critical, potentially life-supporting information? It was too indiscernible to tell if I was even on the right track. It could have been about where they were going that night. Surrounded by limited visuals, constant sounds and unfamiliar voices up and down the hall were the hallmarks of my new world.

Once in a while, light laughter would sharply filter in as someone ran by my door to check on another room. The nurses would be going home soon and after the first few nights, I was becoming more familiar with the shift changes. Time was different now in this new world I was cast into. My clock only ran in eight-hour intervals, three times a day. The knowledge of which was not presented on the dial of a watch, smartphone, or from the chiming of bells in a clock tower. Quietly announced by new shift nurses coming in my room, checking machines and charts, replacing others who had put their backs, compassion, and training into the previous eight, heading out tired. Gregorian time was irrelevant and non-purposeful in my new world, as foreign to me as it was to most anyone outside of some European countries before 1582.

Approaching three weeks after my surgery, my respiratory rate and oxygen levels were dropping, according to my doctors. A lack of sleep, a mind overloaded with stimuli encased in a body pushed to its limits, the drop-off in my breathing ability was not surprising. The irritating and uncomfortable rubber nose cannulas, inserted through my nostrils down to my lungs two weeks ago, were sadly not "pushing" enough air now. Equally concerning was the possible damage being done to my vocal cords if these cannulas stayed for longer than two weeks. There were no notable signs of cyanosis, the condition which can show a blue tinge to the skin, most often signaling a drop off of oxygen saturation near the surface. Though it was obvious to all; the doctors, my parents, and the nursing staff, I was dropping off in that department.

Another sleepless night presented a morning with chairs around my bed, all those involved in my care, now gathered for a conference with my doctors and parents. One more of many that had already taken place over the last three weeks. As my parents listened, looking sad and somber, they were already aware of what the doctors would discuss, learning of the plan the night before. They had already informed me and I knew what the surgeon was going to say as he began to explain what the recommended tracheostomy surgery procedure was and what it hoped to accomplish.

"A tracheostomy should help bring more of the necessary oxygen to heal," the surgeon elaborated. I didn't argue or have that much to say. If it helps, okay, though I wasn't excited about cutting a hole in the front of my neck, bringing more oxygen or not. My neck surgery had left a six-inch scar on the back of my neck already, and I was pretty sure I'd have some nice holes on my forehead and the back of my head from the quarter inch screws drilled into my skull when they were eventually removed. I was beginning to feel like some modern day Frankenstein, just an experiment with all that was taking place, and I still couldn't move after all the drilling, cutting, wrapping, poking with sharp needle objects all over my body, and the stretching of my neck earlier. I was more than tired of operations, scalpels or painful procedures.

This operation was just another revelation to my roller-coaster mind, emotionally charged and wired tight, but feeling equally numb as well. Very hard to explain that particular feeling to someone, unless one has gone through something that was rough, excruciatingly painful and shocking at first, followed by multiple surgeries, bringing the additional pain. Toughest of all was taking that pain with zero painkillers, morphine or anything to cut its dark, harsh and brutish edges. But extreme pain presents opportunities as well, and though not welcome, takes one to a place few have dared to venture, what we might visualize as a hell-like environment. Similar to Hades if one believes in such a place; a body subjected to what seems like torturous procedures and experiences, hurt repeatedly and thoroughly tested through extreme challenges. At the other end of the spectrum; a wishful place, a Mount Olympus-type environment where dreams can come true. In my case, basking in the glow of this heavenly realm, I would visualize my spinal cord somehow magically or divinely fixed, gathering my strength and sitting up, ripping the IVs out my arms, removing the electrode pads from my body and walking out unaided. Never to return and my physique back as it was within six months.

In my current state, I didn't feel like Orpheus, Hercules, Odysseus or Theseus, where I would walk out in the light barely escaping a harrowing experience deep in the bowels of an infinitely dark and dangerous place. Contemplating my life while lying there, I didn't think I would be escaping my personal Hades anytime soon. My mind would roam between these two extremes, depending on different things from procedures to my mood.

My new world three weeks since the accident had now turned into something beyond surreal, where everything I was going through hadn't yet fully sank in or registered, almost like viewing myself from another plane seeing my physical self trapped in a situation I couldn't escape. Where the memories of the event that put me here turned over and over again in my mind, stuffed in-between new revelations or procedures I was undergoing. Broken, bloody and real memories, in a constant, never-ending playback loop.

I'm sure some of you who are reading this have possibly experienced that feeling or know someone who has. A sad situation where your mind is always running hard, processing whatever it can in its broken vessel. Just grabbing at whatever sensory information is available to process and assess, through substantially compromised senses. The data rushed in, mostly unfiltered and not administered in a clear and balanced way.

I wasn't close to functioning at the level of, say, a pilot's perspective when viewing a screen of a target off in the distance, or that of a Buddhist monk's—calm, trained and detached, just looking at life as it changes in front of him. No surprise there, I was down, bound and in pain. In this strange and scary world, I just floated along after encountering that dizzying drop into my personal abyss. I felt like I had taken a kayak down a raging river with no paddle, flipped over the falls and was being washed downstream in my own river Styx, not catching any breaks like drifting ashore or snagging on a limb to stop. In Greek mythology as a God, if you had sworn some great oath on that underworld river and had bro ken a promise, you were punished by paralysis for one year and a day. I wasn't a God, and I didn't break any promises that I knew of, though here I was. I wanted to just halt the machines, the noise, procedures and most of all, the damn paralysis. Let alone go home. Now, I heard another "something that should help" winged my way.

I just smiled and agreed to the tracheostomy. Not thinking, I tried, but couldn't muster a weak "thumbs up." My hands and arms had remained motionless at my sides, unmoving since the night of the accident. Though the memories of using hand gestures and body movements while communicating were still tucked in my mind, still *reflexive* in a sense. This time, the memory had snuck through. Would those memories tucked away in my conscious and sub-conscious be available again someday when I could use them? Only God could answer that.

At this stage, though arm or hand movement wasn't possible, "phantom limb" sensation was apparent to me, roughly from my elbows down to my hands. Wasn't sure what that meant or if that meant anything, the feeling attached to me, but not of me. *Hopefully, someday the feeling would materialize to be real*, I groggily thought.

The orderlies taking me down to surgery arrived later that day. They grabbed the tubes and monitors going with me, unhooking this or that, making sure the long tubes in my veins wouldn't snag on the stretcher's wheels. When everything was safely gathered, they headed toward another part of the hospital, wheeling at a fast pace down a well-lit hallway.

"Busy day," they confided, "lots of surgeries stacked." Whirring by, only able to look up, I noticed the rectangular fluorescent lights flying by seemed a little longer than the ones at the first hospital. As they pushed the stretcher into the operating room, four strangers dressed head to toe in blue, greeted me. They all had green masks over their mouth and nose and were wearing green headgear as well.

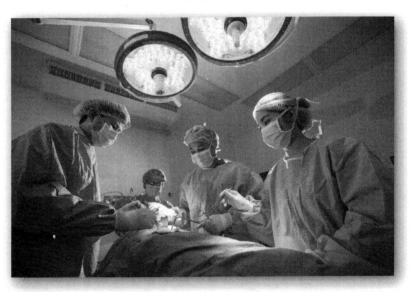

One leaned over my stretcher and started to inject anesthesia into one of the tubes going into my vein. Similar words I had heard several times before greeted my ears as a female voice emptied the syringe. Whispering, "Just relax, this won't hurt and then we'll..." With that, I disappeared once more into the same mute and faceless darkness, greeted by the gatekeeper of my personal abyss.

Trach Talk and Losing Control

"It is better to conquer yourself than to win a thousand battles. Then the victory is yours. It cannot be taken from you, not by angels or by demons, heaven or hell."

---BUDDHA

I WOKE UP, TETHERED TO another machine, one that was pumping oxygen into my lungs forcibly, inflating my chest, then the air rushed out, then inflating again, over and over. Now I was unable to speak. I vaguely recalled that it was one of the side effects of the necessary procedure. Though I had a priceless advantage compared to many— my mother and father were present at the hospital virtually every day, my dad usually after work or very early in the morning on his way to the office. Now that I couldn't verbally communicate, having them available to discuss my procedures and care with the doctors was invaluable. I hadn't slept but a handful of hours over the previous three weeks and was running on a highly compromised breathing and immune system as well. Hopefully, the extra air from the ventilator would help get me back on track. I knew I was in bad shape physically, and my mental stability was starting to wane.

Over the next week, there were several occasions where I would doze off from sheer exhaustion, only to wake suddenly, feeling that I was almost suffocating. It was akin to wearing a straitjacket and being firmly secured to the bed, unable to move anything, with a steel ring anchored around your head with screws, attached to a tight, hard shell torso encasement from your neck down to the waist. Add to this macabre look, a large tube in my neck, pumping in air 24/7, multiple machines beeping this or that and numerous tubes in my veins to complete the picture. I could now only move my eyes and mouth words when the nurse came in. She would lean over if she couldn't understand me, and the "blinking game" would commence, one for yes and two for no.

After a week had passed, they came and took me to another section of the hospital, one with more traumatic and ventilator-dependent patients, who like I, could no longer speak. Human ingenuity would take center stage when the nurses were out of our rooms. Since everyone could only muster screechy-like sounds, it was reminiscent of what one would experience at a bird aviary, or perhaps a jungle section at a zoo with a lot of parrots. Unlike some birds, though, no understandable words came forth, just unintelligible calls. Being a large regional spinal cord center and judging by the varied sounds and bird-like calls I would hear on this wing, there must have been quite a few ventilator-dependent patients and some like I, who had lost the use of their limbs.

From the break of dawn into the wee hours of the night, this sorrowful mix of sounds from the many injured, letting out screeches for help, some much more feeble than others, was the soundtrack of my new life. A heart-wrenching cacophony of desperate calls, unique sounds all commingled, reflecting the confusion, pain, and suffering of those now holding a seat in this hellish orchestra. For those loved ones, like my parents, friends, and family exposed to this, I'm sure it wasn't easy and was incredibly depressing.

The sounds and screeches, all different, would become identifiable to the nurse's over time, serving to get their attention while they were out in the hall or roaming between rooms. It is impossible to convey in words what my call sounded like or resembled, but it worked and was distinguishable from others on this wing. I used it when I was thirsty, uncomfortable and for other reasons; it helped bring me needed relief.

At night, the calls would diminish to some degree from patients like me, quietly wrestling with difficult-to-obtain sleep, to others knocked out by powerful sedatives.

A fresh, new and sad melody of sounds and screeches would greet the mornings as patients woke. One by one the screeches would drop off, as the room's demands were met. Sometimes, there would be new patients added to the unit, judging by the new calls and sounds, some replacing others, their unique sounds no longer present. Hopefully, they were able to make it out to brighter days and fulfilling lives.

I was still having difficulty getting any sleep or beneficial rest. Drifting off, I was still on guard in a sense, a feeling that remained from the first night after the accident, believing that sleep would take away my ability to strictly observe what was happening around me and more importantly, to me. The fact that the doctors and nurses would rush in, never asking if I had any questions, still bothered me immensely, not that I could talk. They sure didn't have the time to figure out what I would attempt to communicate, based on their haste and patient load. It seemed to be one busy unit, and they would quickly make changes here and there to the various machines my body was dependent on and then rush off to see their next patient.

Hours would go by extending into days, where only through sheer exhaustion would I pass out for a few hours, only to quickly awaken. Unable to block out the noise from the beeping of the monitors, the patients calls, my lungs being artificially inflated up and down, the staff coming in unannounced all hours of the day and night, let alone my extreme discomfort, I found it virtually impossible to sleep.

After several weeks of this, I was slipping even further backward, and the sheer toll of sleep deprivation was affecting my already weakened state. The doctors prescribed a sleeping pill, which I reluctantly took, but I still found myself continuing to fight off sleep, as well as the effects of the medication.

This was the beginning of intense hallucinations. Frightening periods where my mind would play wild tricks, seemingly very real during the moments they took place. Fortunately, they never lasted long, mainly occurring when my temperature would start to spike five to six degrees above average. These elevated temperatures would always occur at night and around the same time for several weeks on end. My body had not yet totally adjusted to the paralysis and temperature spikes like this were pretty common for my level of injury, I was later to learn.

Several hours after dinner as my temperature rose, nurses would come in and start the process of packing artificial ice bags on and around my body, from my neck all the way down to my feet. When completed, they would then place what's known as an "ice blanket" on top of me, which is nothing more than a rubber mat connected to what looked like a high-tech air conditioner with cold water circulating throughout. As my temperature rose, literally over 102 degrees on to 103 or 104, many of the ice bags would melt. The nurses would come back into my room about two hours later and start to replace those that had melted, continuing this routine until my fever subsided. It wasn't unusual for me to doze off after they left as the ice helped to bring short-term relief. Then I would quickly awaken, as the clock on the wall opposite of me would start to spin backwards, slowly at first, then faster and faster, till it almost seemed as if it would fly off the wall.

Other occasions, I felt like I was floating out of my body like a human balloon and would find myself bumping up against the ceiling. Never my entire body, just my neck and head detached, floating up, feeling my face brush up against the white paint of the ceiling. Thankfully, during the day through the early evening, until visitors were told to leave, my mother would be at my bedside through the majority of these episodes, promising she wouldn't go anywhere, but I still couldn't let myself find rest. If they were not traveling on business, my father and sister would join her in the early evening after their workday had ended. One early morning on the way to his office, my Dad while leaning down over his mentally compromised son, watched me mouth, *"Night nurse tried to kill me last night."* The nurse wasn't trying to harm me, but in my mind, on more than one night, I sure thought she was.

Beyond that episode, my father and sister didn't witness many of these events, moments that were mostly relegated to afternoons when I would doze off unexpectedly and suddenly wake or at night after visitation hours had ended. Unable to slow my mind down enough to allow much sleep was taking quite a toll on my compromised state and my higher temperature, sleep medication, ventilator and the halo ring on my head were not helping matters either.

Other times upon waking suddenly in the afternoon after falling asleep for a few mere minutes, I would suddenly find myself executing three quick summersaults on the bed, all while my mother was at my bedside. It wasn't easy on her, witnessing what I was going through. It was quite shocking to me; my heart raced uncontrollably at first, the feeling was so real and unnerving. I would catch myself after a short time, knowing it was all in my mind.

Once in awhile, it would feel as if my bed was standing straight up against the wall, nothing to prevent my body from falling out, panicking that I would fall forward, crashing onto the floor. Many times while my temperature rose at night, I would feel as if I was on a lathe, spinning at high speed. With my body completely straight, and screws holding my head still, I could have been filtering in partial memories of woodshop class in my youth making table legs on that high-speed, rotating machine. My mind was starting to lose the battle, the last vestige of control that I had retained and it too, was sadly ebbing away.

I knew I had to come up with something to try to conquer these occurrences of hallucinations and disturbing events. I realized that my health and wellbeing depended on having them stop. How, though? I had never meditated consciously before and was always on the move prior to the accident, never stopping to take any time to unwind mentally. I relied on leisure activities, working out, running, relationships, social events or various forms of media distractions when relaxing after a stressful week. I wasn't sure what to do as I lay there, but one night for whatever reason, I came up with an idea. An idea that I still cannot pin down to this day, as to why I chose it to help me. Hopefully something that just might help me to regain control of my rapidly slipping mental processes.

As the nurses filed out of my room, my entire body encased in ice bags, I knew they most likely wouldn't return for several hours to check on me unless a monitor went off or I initiated contact. I realized this was probably my best opportunity and began to conjure in my mind a large map of the United States. I put a starting point of Philadelphia and picked San Francisco as my destination. As I looked down from a great distance at this enormous map, I pictured myself going cross-country by steam locomotive to the West Coast.

I had decided on San Francisco since I had been to the city numerous times. Several years earlier, while working on an oil tanker running up and down the west coast from Alaska to Panama, one of our key ports was San Francisco. It was a very lucrative opportunity and it only set me back one college semester. I knew I would visit some cool ports and a couple of Latin American countries, so I eagerly went. I knew the states I would cross to get from Philadelphia to the San Francisco Bay and saw them clearly on the map in my mind. Somehow I found myself drawing upon past knowledge and experiences to try and help me through the difficult circumstances I was now facing.

Picture of the American Sun, the oil tanker I was assigned to, whose route was Alaska to Panama. The ship is anchored in Valdez, Alaska picking up crude to discharge to ports south. One can see the beautiful mountains bordering the sound

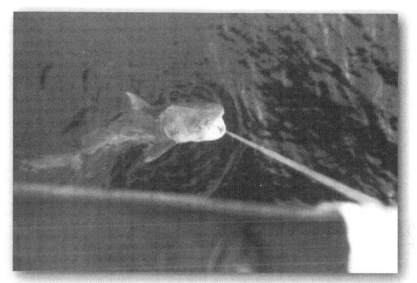

Onboard the American Sun, anchored off the coast of Panama
waiting to discharge Alaskan crude, I decided to pass some time
fishing for shark. I caught a 16-foot Bull Shark, which was quite
an amazing experience. He was subsequently let go.

On my huge mental map of the United States, the goal to win
(mainly regain full control of my mind again) was to stop the train at the
station in San Francisco, after departing from Philadelphia. I closed
my eyes and visualized the train leaving the station in Philadelphia. I
imagined myself as the conductor. I was the only one aboard, and as
my body temperature rose, the train's speed started increasing as well,
something I couldn't control. The locomotive blazed across my mental
map, tearing away from the metaphorical station in Philadelphia. I felt
as if I was on a rocket sled perched on rails that became red-hot as we
flew along them. My mind was spinning, similar to other nights, at a
pace that was overwhelming. Incredibly, after a short time, I realized
the imagery of the wheels on the train appeared to be matching my
spinning mental state at the same rate and speed. In my mind's eye, my
view kept shifting from the map to seeing myself back inside the train
running it. I was trying hard to get it under control, to slow those
wheels down somehow.

In my mind's eye, the train was moving at an incredible rate of speed.

As my mind continued to spin, I began to concentrate harder, working to block out everything going on in my room and keep my focus on that train. I started to notice after much concentration, the spinning of the train's wheels was starting to decrease slightly. I felt a little exhilaration come over me, the first time since my accident, encouraged that the "mental game" I created was producing positive results. I decided to double down and I took my focus to new levels, determined that train and my spinning mind would not win, not this night.

Separating mind from self, looking from afar, I *saw* the train moving across the Plains, the Rockies, into Utah and through the bottom of Nevada. The locomotive was noticeably slower from my efforts though I knew I still didn't have it under full control. I knew there wasn't a lot of distance left once we crossed into California. I increased my focus, knowing this was the moment to break the cycle of out-of-control daily and nightly hallucinations.

I felt a little panic set in. I did not yet feel secure that I could slow the train down enough to stop it in front of the station. A feeling I had, perhaps similar to that experienced by other young, semi-nervous and beginning train conductors on their first run as well. Being my first time running a train, I didn't want to fail. The train was now less than a mile away from the station as it came into my mind's view.

The train station I visualized was similar to this station.

At the last minute, I decided to add something that I thought might help. I envisioned my past girlfriend in Houston (who was easy to focus on) who would be waiting for me at the station in San Francisco. Drifting into the old station, I visualized her in front of the station in a white dress. She was gently waving in what seemed a slower motion, the entire visual noticeably subdued, as if all time had found a more stable and passive place. While viewing the scene, I continued to focus on stopping the train entirely though it was still moving, slowly rolling along, overshooting the station.

I finally brought it to a stop about fifty yards past. I visualized myself jumping down out of the locomotive and running back to the station. I hugged my ex-girlfriend and the imagery ended. The hallucinations and spinning in my mind, which had haunted me for so many nights and days, seemed to be gone.

I lay there afterward contemplating what had just taken place. For the first time in awhile, *I felt I was back in control at least mentally.* I never understood or figured out why I decided to visualize the map, the speeding train, and destination, but somehow it worked.

From that moment on and to this day, I never experienced again those intense, out of control tricks one's mind can play on your psyche when presented with challenging conditions. It worked well for me, and I'm sure many others have used creative imagery to accomplish a goal or to help move beyond difficult times in their lives. Daydreaming, hypnosis, and focused meditation, among other techniques, have proved helpful to many others as well to assist in the process of visualizing a brighter future, a more stable path, beyond where they are now.

Regaining control of my mind made my ability to move forward much more realistic. Most amazing to me was that immediately following the visualization technique, I began to make greater progress. I found myself sleeping better and my ability to cope and move on significantly improved. I have no doubt it was due to consciously shifting my mind's focus to overcome what I couldn't resolve through conventional practices or means. That feeling of having some control over our situation, however small, helps us begin the process of chipping away at our misfortunes, hopefully contributing to brightening our way ahead.

Let the Progress Begin

"It is our attitude at the beginning of a difficult task which, more than anything else, will affect its successful outcome."

—WILLIAM JAMES

GOING INTO DECEMBER, THE THERAPISTS working with me had started a new therapy regimen to help build up my diaphragm muscles. The exercise program would hopefully enable me to breathe without the aid of a ventilator. Fortunately, I was now able to have what's known as a "talking trach," replacing the other one, now allowing me to communicate verbally. How much easier it was to have demands met, no longer eye blinks, mouthed words or screeches to get relief.

My upper chest muscles were mostly paralyzed, making breathing more difficult. It was a pretty simple program therapy-wise, but highly effective in what it would eventually accomplish. I wanted the ability to breathe on my own, to once again be free of ventilators or machines, and hopefully, these exercises would enable that. To start the diaphragm-building program, the therapists would transfer me onto a table, about eighteen inches high off the ground. Each table was covered with a two-inch thick exercise mat on its surface, upon which they would position me flat and straight, my arms and legs together. It wasn't easy to transfer me. I am 6'2" tall, and I still had the halo ring around my skull and the restrictive vest, making the process more difficult.

The therapists performed some preliminary tests to gauge my post-injury breathing ability. After the initial evaluation was complete, they would begin the exercises by lying flat sandbags on my diaphragm that varied in five, ten and twenty pound increments. This program was something that I could relate to; it was my first exercise program since entering the hospital that involved my participation physically. It was quite a moment. I had enjoyed working out before my accident, and that feeling of testing myself again on a physical level was welcomed wholeheartedly.

I started out with twenty pounds laid across my stomach, feeling no discomfort or effort in breathing. We moved rather quickly up to forty pounds. With this amount of weight, they wanted me to breathe in and out for about twenty minutes as my diaphragm became accustomed to the strain, slowly building up these muscles. After the first session, I noticed my muscles felt sore in my stomach area, not so much on the surface, but internally. This program wasn't easy by any stretch and was tiring. I was working out, though, something I had enjoyed before my injury and although it wasn't the same, it was still based on my abilities alone. While limited in scope compared to my prior workouts, it was still a step in the right direction and helped contribute to my positive mindset at this time. Each step forward, no matter how small it seems, is one step that wasn't made the day or week before. Though I could bench press 320 pounds with free weights before my accident and press 230 pounds over my head, I focused on what remained at this time to work on, and it felt good.

At the next day's session, I felt pretty recovered and asked to add twenty more pounds to the forty I had used the day before. I ended up doing the exercise for thirty minutes this time. Each day for the following two weeks I was in therapy, I continued to build those muscles by increasing the weight, and trying to extend the time. My muscles were sore every time, but by therapy the next day, they were ready to go again. Afterward, I would be wheeled back to the cafeteria, eat, and then be transferred back into bed for the night.

Two more weeks eventually passed, and I continued my daily and nightly regimen. At the end of this period, I was starting to surprise the physical therapists with the amount of weight I requested and how well I could now breathe with my injury. Eventually, my diaphragm muscles were strong enough to place 110 pounds of weight across them for close to an hour. According to the therapists, this was the highest amount of weight used for this therapy on one's abdomen they had witnessed a patient doing with my type of injury. It felt good that I was able to build my diaphragm to that extent, and I was more than happy with the outcome.

The best news was not relying on a machine to breathe anymore, and the tracheostomy was finally removed. I was grateful to no longer have it, and for those who haven't been able to get away from one, my heart and prayers are with you. For people with quadriplegia, strong diaphragm muscles are critical for respiration. By developing mine to the extent I did, enabled me to regain about eighty percent breathing capacity of what a healthy, non-disabled adult male my size would have. Even to this day, I have been able to avoid many of the respiratory ailments such as pneumonia, colds and chest congestion that can often be experienced by many with my injury. One reason is strong diaphragm muscles.

Having conquered my hallucinations, breathing on my own, and moving forward with therapy, my outlook improved. Instead of dwelling on the what-ifs, all the unknowns in a negative light, I began to ask the doctors and nurses more questions about my condition, to learn more about my injury. I had never taken a biology or anatomy course in college, let alone high school, so I was "very green" concerning everything involving paralysis, and was learning along the way. That was okay; I was moving forward.

Rest came more easily now that my mind was under control. The fear and uncertainty of falling asleep no longer bothered me. As a result, I had more energy and looked forward to getting to rehabilitation. I had improved enough to be moved to another unit, one where those patients deemed "strong enough" could begin more stringent physical therapy.

Even more exciting, I was stable enough to be allowed by the doctors to go home by ambulance for about six hours to celebrate Christmas with my family at home, as long as I was back by eight o'clock. It wasn't a lot of time after being away for almost two months, but it was a great gift and lifted my spirits.

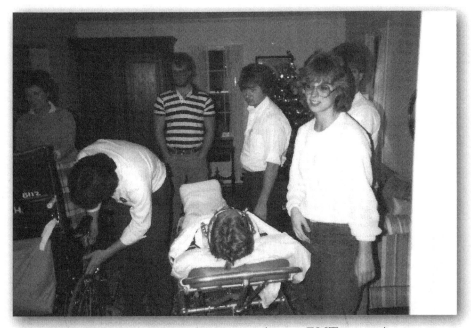

Wheeled into my parent's living room by two EMTs preparing my manual chair for transfer. Pictured L-R: my mother, an EMT adjusting my chair, my brother Chris, an EMT watching the progress, my brother Paul partially blocked by my sister Melinda on the right.

I was elated to go home, if only for a brief time, and knew I was far from stable enough for overnight. I looked forward to being home with my family, seeing the pets and having Christmas with all of them. It wasn't easy (and not inexpensive) for my parents to arrange, but by far it was the best present they could have dreamed up. Just one more thoughtful thing among hundreds they have done over the years for their children.

Pictured: my siblings in the background, a college girlfriend standing
on my right and my maternal grandmother on my left.

Six hours later, the ambulance came back, and it was off to my
room in the rehabilitation hospital in Center City. I didn't want to
leave, and the time seemed to pass too quickly, though I knew there
wasn't a choice. Hopefully, I could be back home soon, and it wasn't
easy saying goodbye. Thankfully, no one broke down crying. I'm
sure I most likely would have had some tears in my eyes, had someone burst out. I smiled, added a few quick comments of thanks and
that I'd see them here again soon, as my parents and grandmother
leaned over to kiss the top of my head. The ambulance crew then
started heading for the front door. I had already been transferred
back to the stretcher, and my manual chair was being taken out to
the ambulance by one of my siblings. It was wonderful to make it
back for the holidays, though short and I'll never forget those special
moments.

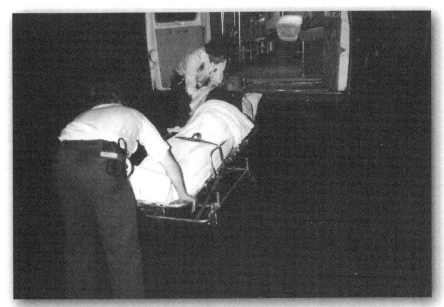

Transferred back onto the stretcher and into the ambulance
for the return trip to the rehabilitation hospital.

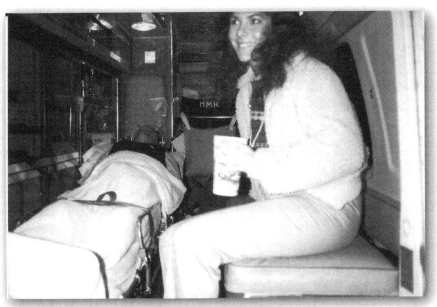

Accompanied by college girlfriend back to the hospital.

The New Year came and went in the rehabilitation center. I didn't make any resolutions, though I felt I had turned the last page on what was a very roller coaster year. Not that the New Years opening chapter had started off with a lot of certainties, but I felt at least its opening was moving in a positive direction. The previous year had begun like an exciting, fun-filled and romantic adventure, the pages recounting an incredible college senior year. Starting with a spring break in Cozumel, graduating, and in the fall, accepting a position with a Fortune 50 company.

Spring break at a hotel/resort in Cozumel with
Eric and Al, two close college friends.

Walking across the stage and accepting my diploma at
Texas A&M from the University president.

A graduation picture, that was taken shortly after the diploma
ceremony. Pictured from L-R: my girlfriend at the time, my paternal
grandmother, and my mother. My father is taking the picture.

Afterward, we all went to dinner to celebrate. I was glad I was done with course work but had left behind many good friends and memories. The first three-quarters of my college graduation year were bright and full of promise. As we talked, catching up with my parents and grandmother, little did I realize what a nightmare I would be facing in the not too distant future.

The New Rehab

"As human beings, our greatness lies not so much in being able to remake the world... as in being able to remake ourselves."

– MAHATMA GANDHI

I WAS HALFWAY THROUGH MY rehabilitation process. After some discussion with my doctors and family, I learned that I was stable enough to transfer to a new rehabilitation center to begin two more months of physical and occupational therapy. The new rehab where I was going was associated with the regional spinal cord hospital, which performed my surgery. It was time for me to undergo a more intensive treatment program than the previous hospital provided. Several days later, I transferred by ambulance to my new destination. My family helped to move my clothes and supplies to my new bedroom, and no longer would it be private. Instead, I would share it with three other patients, all of whom had their own unique spinal cord injury and circumstances. Try to imagine a large room with four beds, one in each corner and everyone having their own dresser and TV. The bedroom areas were separated by curtains suspended on a track mounted on the ceiling, which wrapped around each patient location. The layout provided the barest of privacy and would be my new home for the next three months. I grew to know my roommates and their families well. I became good friends with an Occupational Therapist named Jayne. As she ranged my arms, we would talk, laugh and have fun. She was a beautiful person, not only caring, but truly a giving individual. My family liked her very much, and we continued to stay friends after I was discharged.

Each night as we all settled in, the sounds of four different televisions would fill the room, slightly above the chatter of visitors. After visitation hours had ended, everyone's would stay on for hours, the audio of the program you were viewing intermingled with others. Around one in the morning, the last TV would go off. Sharply at six am, multiple aides would fill the room to get everyone showered and dressed. Then I would be wheeled to the cafeteria for a quick breakfast and parked at an open table until an aide became available to help me. Unable to feed myself, I would end up patiently waiting, sometimes for a half hour or more. Gazing around the cafeteria, I would watch others eat who could use their hands and arms independently. Unable to participate, I found this part of my day incredibly vexing. Eventually, an aide would come over and ask what I wanted to eat from the available choices and join the line waiting to be served.

When they returned, I would quickly eat, before being taken to therapy, parked inside the treatment room to wait till the therapist had finished up with their previous patient. The therapists were caring and conscientious and after two hours of therapy had passed, another aide would show up to bring me to the cafeteria for lunch. I would wait for assistance, order, then back to therapy—the same routine as in the morning session. Once afternoon therapy was over, it was back to the cafeteria, parked at another table for dinner.

Pictured doing a weight shift. This night, my friend
Max assisted while my grandmother observes. My
father is not in the view due to my leg-rests.

As you can imagine, a typical day would present a constant, mind-jarring sequence of steps, requiring great patience and total dependence on others. Patience was one trait among several I had to learn and accept early on. I had not yet been fitted for an electric power chair but was more than ready. Getting manually taken everywhere in the wheelchair was extremely trying. The therapists who had been working with me had taken the various measurements needed for an electric chair that could accommodate my needs. They would end up having to compile quite a lot of data, the mechanics necessary for someone with my level of injury and body size. The electric chair would allow me independent movement and opportunities that only a power chair could offer. I would later learn that the entire process would take many months from start to finish. Though the process was long, it was well worth the wait, I assure you.

Therapy continued at this new rehabilitation facility until my spinal cord had healed enough to remove the halo and the supporting vest. As the screws were removed from my skull, the halo ring was eventually lifted off. They held my head steady while a nurse carefully attached a stiff rubber collar around my neck. Then they removed the vest. It felt good to have this very restrictive hard shell and steel ring removed after so many months of being held rigidly in its grasp! I would still require the neck collar for an additional three months. My neck was fragile from non-movement, and the collar would provide the necessary support to protect it from bending too far, too quickly. A few days later, the pressure and pain from the screws was starting to subside, though it would take time to no longer be aware of the Halo ring's former presence. Tissue and nerve re-growth had to occur first. The telltale holes on the sides of my temple and the back of my head would eventually heal, as would the long scar on the back of my neck. They remain faintly visible, serving as reminders of earlier challenges and events I had faced and survived.

Having the halo and vest off was wonderful. I had begun a regimen of very mild therapy on my neck to regain some of my strength and mobility. It was a little unnerving at first trying to build it up; not only was it frail, there was no way I wanted to re-injure it and have to start everything over. The therapy started out very slowly, testing my neck's flexibility by moving my head up and down a couple of inches forward then backward, basically to the limitations imposed by the neck collar. I noticed it would become extremely sore and fatigued very quickly, and the therapy was pretty painful. Said with a little humor, heads are heavy, and mine was no exception.

The doctors assured me that movement was now possible, but due to the fractured vertebrae they had repaired, full mobility and flexibility would not completely return. I began building my neck back up, extending its flexibility while strengthening it in the process. After several weeks of some pretty grueling therapy, my flexibility and neck strength had increased. My collar was removed after two and a half months, a full two weeks ahead of what the doctors expected.

In my mind, another milestone had been reached; my neck was no longer encumbered and restrained. Five and a half months since the accident and I was now able to move it on my own finally. How long ago that seemed at the time. The neck collar had been hot and irritating, as most who have had to wear one can attest. I couldn't use my hands to adjust it if needed, scratch underneath it or reposition a cloth barrier between my skin and the rubber, making my experience that much harder. Tough lessons to absorb, losing all ability to perform the many subtle, almost subconscious movements all able-bodied people do to alleviate discomfort.

The only way to experience what it is like is to remain immobile, for an hour or so. Try not to scratch your head, nose or body during the entire process and then count how many times just in one hour you felt that itch or discomfort somewhere on you. Now multiply that inability to scratch that itch, consciously or not, by the many hours in a day. That experience will provide you a good idea of how annoying this was. Fortunately, I noticed with time, that if something itched, often that feeling subsided in a very short period. Of course, this only refers to minor things, not if one is consumed with poison ivy for example, and fortunately, I never was after the accident.

I knew my rehabilitation and monotonous routines would not last forever and looked forward to the evenings in the company of family and friends. Two weeks later, I was allowed to go home. I could continue therapy at a physical rehabilitation center nearby. I was ready to leave; six months had now passed since the night of my accident, making my discharge a beautiful thing.

Home Sweet Home

"Love begins by taking care of the closest ones—the ones at home."

–Mother Teresa

"Where we love is home—home that our feet
may leave, but not our hearts."

--Oliver Wendell Holmes

WHAT A DIFFERENCE IN ENVIRONMENT a home represents to everyone who has been away, for any period. No matter the reason for our absence, reacquainting ourselves once again with the familiar rooms, smells, faces, and sounds, for the vast majority of us, has an uplifting and rejuvenating effect. I sure appreciated being back. Those who have been in a hospital for a stretch know that real healing takes place better on our home turf, hopefully with family and friends if possible. A better chance to rest and home-cooked food sure helps! I was now more weathered, tested and tired, but I had made it back. Healing my body and mind would just take time.

I was extremely fortunate that a very helpful attendant who had cared for me in the rehabilitation center accepted a live-in position in my parents' home after I was discharged. We got along well, and she would be responsible for getting me up in the morning and putting me in bed at night. All in all, it was a pretty good deal for her; she could live with us in return for helping and continue her college courses toward her nursing degree during the day. For my parents and me, it was a virtual lifesaver.

Coming home accompanied by an excellent, well-trained assistant to care for me alleviated a lot of stress in trying to find help. Before my arrival, my parents had a very long wooden ramp constructed and installed at their home, complete with a turn to enable wheelchair access through the front door. It was quite an undertaking, but the only real possibility at the time, the back entry door into the house required climbing eight steps to get in. The ramp was over forty feet long, then turned at ninety degrees, requiring an additional fifteen feet in length to gain access to the front door. If one were viewing from the street, you would think they had built a large model airplane strip or skateboard ramp; it was so large. This long ramp would serve as the entryway into their house until the summer. Three months later, a new door was cut into the side of their home, leading into their relatively large den on the first floor, which would now serve as my new bedroom. A separate driveway was put in the side yard, complete with a wooden deck and ramp to gain access to the new entrance.

My parents' thoughtful renovations to provide me a private entrance into my bedroom, along with a deck and separate parking area to accommodate my oversized van, was pure, unconditional love. They had made a previously inaccessible situation accessible, and they went to great lengths to provide me a modicum of privacy to the best of their ability. The changes to their house were quite intensive. Their previous laundry room would now have to be redesigned into a shower, large enough to accommodate my shower chair. The washer and dryer would have to be relocated in their basement. My parents' home was forever altered; their sacrifice to accommodate my disability needs cannot be overstated. Their love and support, from my childhood up through the tragic accident to now, never wavered. They always put my siblings and me first. A true testament of parental love and for this, I am eternally grateful.

My parents never let me know if they were ever overwhelmed by my accident, including all they had to accomplish to make my return home possible. I'm sure, though, through many eyes when viewing my new situation, the future ahead for me appeared very daunting and seemingly insurmountable. The sheer magnitude, depth, and complexity of my needs required an extensive list of things that had to be accomplished first just to get me physically home. All the doorways on the first floor had to be widened to accommodate my chair. I required a lot of medical equipment, from a shower chair, hospital bed, to a transportation van with a mechanical lift and a raised roof to accommodate my over-sized wheelchair. The medical bills, insurance claims, hiring additional assistants, therapists, along with other concerns would have to be addressed and would be ongoing.

My parents had their already busy lives uprooted since the night of my accident, a severely injured son now home added to the mix. For one who is physically or mentally challenged, though their lives will be difficult and challenging, the lives of those closest to them are also significantly affected as well. They, like you, are also faced with daunting tasks, stress and challenging periods ahead, often making great sacrifices for your well-being, as my parents did for me. If fortunate enough to have loving parents like I do, they shoulder the greatest grief of all. Now that I was home, in a sense, it was easier for me to move on if I so chose, and look beyond my physical limitations. I realized early on, if I showed any pain or sorrow, it was also their hurt and sadness as well. I worked hard to prove I would be okay.

Finding Acceptance &
Personal Reflections

*"Though I was paralyzed from the shoulders
down, I still had relevance in this world."*

ACCEPTANCE OF MY DISABILITY WAS difficult several times after the acci-dent while in the hospital. I had a few thoughts of not wanting to live this way. Nothing too serious, just brief moments of sadness in the beginning as the awareness of my condition and extreme limitations sank in. I was young and like most young adults was more focused on my current, hor-rific situation, having few thoughts concerning my future. I had no idea what the future held or what lay ahead, as few of us in life ever do.

I decided, early on, that acceptance of my injury was the route I would take. That did not mean an *acceptance* that I was down for the count or I would give up on life. I knew the magnitude or severity of any obstacles I might face by going forward would be indeterminable, until after the fact. I would have to go with the flow, and whatever I encountered I'd have to deal with as best as possible. I knew this new life would be a major challenge, but I also felt it would present opportunities. Some of them I would never have signed up for voluntarily and revolved around my in-jury. The least appealing alternative was just giving up, and I knew that would never sit well with me. I still wanted to have a life and felt inside that I still had a lot to live for, let alone prove to myself.

Finding acceptance of my disability was paramount, though; without that, it would hinder my ability to move forward. I was still frail when I arrived home. I would find myself dozing off during the day and knew that wasn't me, sitting around in a weak and fog-like state. After some research, conversations with other doctors and getting second opinions concerning medications, I started weaning myself off a list of pills pre-scribed to me when I left. I started taking many more vitamins and using herbal supplement alternatives, taking away all the fog and tiredness I had initially, bringing back greater clarity and focus into my day and life. Plus, at least mentally, I had myself back. I am not suggesting that discontinu-ing prescribed medications your doctor recommends without knowing all the facts, is a good idea. Doing independent research and getting second, third and other objective opinions is a better alternative. Knowledge set me free and enabled me to move forward faster than what would have been the case had I continued with the prescribed medications upon discharge.

I also realized I could still have a fulfilling life, and one with pur-pose. I wanted to prove not only to myself but my friends, family and the co-workers I would eventually work with *though I was paralyzed from the shoulders down, I still had relevance in this world.* I had my pride and coupled with hope; ambition. Acceptance of my paralysis would at times be vexing, difficult and trying beyond one's imagination. Ultimately, my happiness and successes would be up to me. My life events and chal-lenges could either be met with sorrow or viewed as just another test. Hopefully, my steps forward would be in the direction I envisioned.

My journey had now started. I was home, my health and injury stabilized. I continued to educate myself on new, objectively oriented medical studies on everything from vitamins and supplements to new discoveries in spinal cord research, among other breakthroughs in sci-ence and medicine. I also wanted to start building my physique to the degree that my paralysis would allow and continue with my therapy lessons. I wanted to do my therapy at my home (instead of an outpatient facility) and eventually purchased a muscle stimulation bike after saving some funds. Insurance would not cover the cost, but I knew it was important to build my leg muscles back up by using attached electrodes that would keep my legs from atrophying. For my arms, I eventually had an assistant help me make slings that I could pull up and down with a little assistance. Also, I would learn to find acceptance, adapt and accomplish my goals by training assistants to help me. Fortunately, verbalizing was not a difficult thing for me. Some would say I voiced my thoughts and opinions quite readily, requested or not. Having vocal abilities has made my journey so much easier, for which I am grateful.

Though I had been battered physically and my emotional self, rocked violently, I had hoped and prayed for calmer waters. On the horizon of my new life, I was similar to a boat in distress trying to ride out a terrible storm.

I felt tossed around in my mind and finding calm was difficult at first.

I didn't like being paralyzed, and I'm sure anyone who is, doesn't either. Now that I was home, and we were entering May, it was saddening to realize many of the things I enjoyed doing were no longer possible. I could vividly remember spending my summers water-skiing and going to the shore. By the time I graduated, my family had enjoyed waterskiing on a used boat my father had purchased years earlier. We would have fun on the water every summer and bring friends along occasionally, and many were taught to ski as well. My father was an excellent captain, calmly managing a 16-foot boat loaded with noisy and energetic participants.

Enjoying one of many runs on a slalom ski.

I also missed driving my used Spider Fiat five-speed convertible. I purchased the car after graduation. I enjoyed having a fast convertible and would keep the top down most of the time, weather permitting.

Parked outside work on the outskirts of Houston during
the summer months following graduation.

Eventually I encountered calmer places in my mind, and as a result, I was more ready to set sail and journey on. I ventured out with a strong understanding that rough times and stormy waters most likely lay ahead. I felt more prepared; the many months in the hospitals and rehabilitation centers had taught me a lot. I also realized I was more thoughtful and focused after all I had been through since the accident. More *seaworthy*, in a sense, and able to navigate my uncharted territory ahead, like our sea explorers of old. Reminiscent of Leif Ericsson, Magellan, Vasquez, Columbus and the many others who had set out across waters unknown. Something inside was driving each one of them to undertake the journey. In all modesty, I would never compare myself to these great adventurers, though my journey ahead was uncertain, like theirs. I was going, though, like them, knowing I didn't have any other choice.

My personal rewards were not to be new lands or vast riches, but merely the wisdom and experiences I would gain along the way. In life, we have all faced voyages into an unfamiliar and challenging territory, some of our journeys more trying than others. With experience and successful outcomes weathering difficult times, we learn to navigate once more what initially looked quite daunting and foreboding. We find ourselves in hindsight thinking, *"wow that was much easier than I thought it would be!"*

There are challenges we undertake of our choosing. Climbing a mountain, earning a degree and exploring remote parts of the world attest to the human desire to challenge one's self. For most, due to this innate quality to go on, humankind on average will look to get back up after stumbling. Many will brush themselves off, and someone once said, "How can we learn to get up if we don't fall along the way?" Our perceptions and mindset directly impact the choices we make—the more we believe in ourselves, the more positive we try to be, the easier it will be to move forward. How else could the human species have survived and thrived for thousands of years when faced with so many catastrophic events? Many people test that trait all their lives, that inner drive to once again prove something to themselves, often into their eighties, nineties and beyond!

In many cases, there are lessons in our lives that were the last thing we wanted. But that's the route we ended up on, horrific things and situations that often we can't begin to understand, feeling, w*hy us or why them?* Not to mention, our individual struggles to find acceptance for questions that have no answers or answers that hardly explain. How we choose to view our fate or destiny is up to every one of us. Just maybe, hopefully, there are brighter horizons ahead for us, than from where we just came.

For some, acceptance comes with time. Like a gray fog that first engulfs and through experiences, begins to lift—making it easier to view and assess our situation with greater clarity and vision. After some victories overcoming difficult periods under my belt, my confidence to continue forward grew as well, helping to take away some of the traces of self-doubt that lingered at first. Acceptance freed me to move forward, no longer fettered with the sorrow and pain that trag-edy brings. Hopefully, those facing what seem to be insurmountable challenges will find someday that you are ready to move forward again. Finding acceptance and moving on empowers you to achieve those dreams and goals you had established before your setback.

Learning to Adapt &
Finding Patience & Peace

*"My paralysis now required me to take a long pull off the canteen
known as "adaptability" more often. Tasting foreign and bitter at
first, nothing like the fresh waters of my previous existence."*

WHEN FORCED TO DRINK THIS bitter water due to unforeseen events
related to my accident, it was not pleasing to my palate, requiring time
and effort to accept. Things were now more challenging when I was
faced with unexpected situations, making my "personal river" flow
slower and more chaotic than before. Occasionally it was due to assistants who were unable to make it to work, the random equipment
malfunction, health setbacks and a myriad of other things related to my
injury. I tried to be as proactive as possible on the front-end, to minimize these events, though you can never plan for everything, as we all
know. My new circumstances also required a higher level of flexibility
on my part than before. Before the accident, though I had exposure to
adapting to typical daily events, it didn't play as consuming a role as it
did now in my day-to-day life.

Over time, I learned to approach unexpected problems from many
more perspectives in my mind than I ever had to before. Learning
adaptability helped me not to get caught up "in the moment" as often,

providing a stronger ability to think through the issue and resolve it as best as I could. When faced with unexpected and adverse events, I tried not to draw them to me but strived to hold them at a distance. I worked on not allowing them to absorb me, bemoaning what I felt was my bad fortune. Instead, I worked to visualize beyond the unexpected as just another test or challenge to solve. Not to say I wasn't annoyed, let alone disappointed when dealing with an issue, like all of us. Of course in life, some unexpected disappointments and setbacks are seemingly impossible to move forward from afterward. It doesn't make our situation any easier if negative emotions overwhelm us on top of it.

~

"I hadn't known how difficult patience could be before my accident, though my understanding grew, becoming a steady companion in my life. Journeying with me ever since that memorable night; we are inseparable it seems."

Visualize yourself strapped in a wheelchair unable to move, except from the shoulders up, arms and legs motionless. Imagine that you're thirsty or perhaps hungry and no one is home to give you something to eat or drink. Some time later a phone call comes in, informing you that the assistant scheduled to arrive next, is unable due to car trouble. Upon calling a backup, you find that they cannot get to your house for several hours. So you wait longer than you thought when needs arise. There isn't any choice. If that doesn't teach one about patience, try it for a week, let alone a year or longer. Those who are physically challenged or have to rely on assistance for having needs met can relate to this I'm sure.

Patience is further learned and experienced, often during times of inclement weather conditions like snow and ice, a very common occurrence in the northeastern United States. Often, when faced with weather that presented challenging driving conditions, my assistant coverage was tough to arrange. It wasn't unusual for an assistant to show up an hour to five hours late to get me up in the morning, depending on the severity or magnitude of the storm. Other times might involve an assistant calling out due to flu or sickness, a death in the family, automobile issues on to a myriad of many other reasons. I made efforts to minimize the impact of unexpected situations, though sometimes the strongest of efforts were to no avail.

My compassion for others grew, as I was now able to have a much deeper understanding of what others who are living with disabilities, disease, and other debilitating conditions, go through. Finding peace with my disability was harder and came much later. It would be marked by fits and starts, sometimes due to unexpected setbacks with my health and the numerous obstacles one regularly encounters with this injury. For me, though, peace came with acceptance.

Hopefully, others with complicated lives reading this book will find some version of peace for themselves. Enjoying life and all its wonderments, thankful for what you have and not consumed by what you lack.

Setting Goals

Choosing a profession and pursuing a career was an important goal in my mind. Doing so and having severe physical limitations, I knew it wouldn't be easy. I wanted to get back into some career that would be fun and challenging. The question was: What? How? I determined after being home for several months, that to ultimately reach my goal of having a career, there would have to be smaller goals and hurdles that I would have to clear first. I realized there would be setbacks and disappointments along the way and how I perceived things internally would help determine how well I could move forward. Beyond an hour or two of therapy a day, I had plenty of time to spend contemplating my life. I was also aware early on that ultimately I was in control of my destiny to a great degree, and how far I would go was up to me.

I had read somewhere that, *"One either rides out to meet their destiny, or they are trampled by the stampede of fate."* Personally, I now felt more ready to ride out into the world again and see what I could gain by trying.

By setting the goals I wanted to accomplish, I had something to work toward and keep me busy. I knew my starting point; now I had to determine what separated me from my ultimate goal. I had to be realistic; I was paralyzed, which would preclude me from a lot of things that would require being able-bodied. That was easy, determining what I couldn't do that required mobility. What I was capable of was what I needed to figure out. I didn't have a long work history, and I had no idea what was possible. I still felt outgoing and confident, and my health was stable. Fortunately, I had my mental faculties intact. I considered what I might enjoy doing and came up with the idea of being a money manager in the financial services industry.

I didn't know anyone personally in this field, whether family, friends or neighbors. Not one person. How to get there? Not only a challenging field to be successful in, it would also be a journey in which I had no familiarity or any sources. Though to me, a money management career seemed plausible to pursue. The beauty was it didn't require me to be able-bodied, at least in my eyes.

Though my career choice did present a path and destination where many things weren't even close to being mapped. My "map" almost felt reminiscent of our country's map of the west, before Lewis and Clarke's expedition in 1804-1806, mostly covered with dense and uncertain forests, with no sure way to get to my final destination.

I knew my journey ahead would be uncertain.

My journey can't begin to compare to the hardships Lewis and Clarke endured, and I wouldn't be fending off arrows or wild animals, though I had no idea what lay ahead. The internal map I envisioned in my mind had two destinations on it already. One of the destinations I had already reached; home and now out of the hospital, stabilized, though paralyzed and realized, not enough was going on in my life. After much consideration, I began to visualize what the destination on the other side of this unmapped forest might hold for me. A non-metaphorical city, an established financial firm within, that was hopefully hiring new stockbrokers/money managers or at least interviewing for positions. I knew I had to set smaller goals first, goals that would require a lot of thought, planning, and preparation to have a chance of getting there. I knew I was pursuing a career in a highly competitive industry and thought it would hold my interest, something that was important to me. I enjoyed learning and keeping up on the news, markets and world events, which would help satisfy this desire for knowledge.

The career also meant that it was always evolving, from new companies coming public, to those leaving their indelible mark on the world, like Alphabet, Apple, Facebook, Microsoft, Tesla, and the Virgin Group, among many others. The stock and bond markets around the world were always moving and changing, never static in nature and I couldn't see myself getting bored. I also knew I would be interacting with many new people along the way, hopefully developing clients who lived in different locales with diverse backgrounds and stories. Growing up in many different states and towns throughout my life, I looked forward to reconnecting to some degree with all these different locations, even if only on the phone as their money manager. This career would also offer me exposure to states and cities where I had never lived or visited, gaining new understandings and knowledge there as well.

Though it was ambitious, I had virtually nothing to lose trying beyond my time, something I already felt I had too much abundance of and wasn't utilizing to my full capacity. I decided to aim high and the field I chose to pursue cost me little to attempt and wouldn't leave an impact financially if I failed.

I broke my larger goal to be a money manager down to four smaller goals that I felt were necessary for a chance to be hired in the industry. I knew I had to employ and train a support staff that I could rely on to meet my needs, not only physically but in a fast-paced and challenging work environment as well. I would also require a transport van to carry my heavy power chair back and forth to work, and chose a powerful Ford van with a heavy-duty lift and tie-down. This goal also required a good driver, since they were not only responsible for my safety but the safety of everyone else on the road. Don't forget the little details within a goal. An accident caused by an inexperienced or poorly trained driver could have set back my ultimate goal by months or worse; placed either of us or others in the hospital. A destination I had no inclination to return to if I could help it. I realized attention to detail would be important in any of the smaller goals I established.

I reasoned I also needed additional coursework that was more specific to the financial service and brokerage industry. Although I had a Bachelor's of Science in Economics, as well as many other business-related courses, I realized that alone most likely wasn't enough. I decided to attend night classes, two times a week, to help me prepare for the brokerage license test, required in the industry to trade securities. I also took other higher-level courses at night in economics, investing and finance. I subscribed to various publications and magazines, to learn more about the financial markets and individual companies.

I knew additional preparation in interviewing and handling potential employers' questions in this industry would be helpful. I had never applied to a brokerage firm before and wasn't even sure what they were looking for, or if they even thought I was qualified enough to be considered. Physically, I couldn't put in trades independently, and traveling long distances to meet new prospects to try and develop them into clients would be tough. I determined that participating in practice interviews to hone my answers to questions I might be asked would be helpful.

Some goals were easier to achieve than others. I found that it helped to list each goal individually and then determine what needed to be accomplished to succeed at each one. Then I recommend keeping daily or weekly notes and continually examining your progress. To break it down, I provided four steps below.

Set goals that are stepping stones that will help you reach your primary objective.

- List each goal individually.
- Determine what needs to be accomplished to succeed at each goal.
- Examine regularly your progress with each goal.
- Evaluate all the goals you have established and how well they are contributing to the achievement of your ultimate goal.

Starting a Career

⌒

*"Don't be trapped by dogma – which is living with the
results of other people's thinking. Don't let the noise of others'
opinions drown out your inner voice. And most important,
have the courage to follow your heart and intuition."*

—STEVE JOBS, FORMER APPLE CEO, 2005
COMMENCEMENT ADDRESS, STANFORD UNIVERSITY

THOUGH I WANTED TO BE a stockbroker/money manager and had set goals, I still had to complete them. After three months at home with my goals not yet complete, I felt very much like an isolated retiree. I wasn't used to this much slower paced environment after living a life prior that was always full of events and activities. I was seeing friends, doing things with family, taking my girlfriend out, and going to out-patient therapy at a local rehabilitation hospital, but it wasn't enough. This sedentary lifestyle was taking a toll, and getting my goals in place was taking more time than I envisioned going in.

With my physical limitations and only a skeletal assistant support structure in place, the entire process of becoming a stockbroker seemed daunting. I knew the job market was difficult enough even before my injury, having graduated during one of the worst recessions in the previous thirty years.

In a game of poker, dropping out of the hand you were dealt may only cost you an ante or pot. This was my life on the table now, with higher stakes involved, and dropping out didn't have much appeal. This was a hand that I had to play, relying on past hands and skills I had already learned in the game of life. Sometimes, tough hands we're dealt in life turn out better than we initially thought. That was what I was shooting for with the one I had just drawn and would work hard to play it well.

Like the popular poker game Texas Hold 'Em, the very best players can occasionally take what appears to be a losing hand and emerge victorious. Often they rely on intelligence, guts, and instinct to pull off a difficult win. As with most professional players, rarely do you see a player throw in his hand say "I give up," feeling sorry they participated, walk away and never try again. I tried to project a sense of optimism to others concerned with my well-being that my hand was better than it seemed.

I wanted to prove to myself that I could compete in the world of high finance and that my injury would not define me. I would try to make my injury serve me going forward. For instance, I had to verbalize everything from the simplest to the most complex of requests to manage my care and needs, requiring a greater level of communication. I had to try harder, think clearer, and look ahead further. So many things had to go right, be in place for me, just to get on a level playing field with able-bodied, sharp and hungry college graduates. Many new graduates were hitting the job market at the same time as me, along with many others with more experience in various business endeavors. Based on what I read, which was mostly just broad perspective views in papers, quite a few grads were considering a brokerage career and wanted their piece of Wall Street, much like me.

Brokerage firms weren't in the habit of hiring people without a solid background in the industry or at the very least an undergraduate degree. Most companies preferred to hire someone with a graduate degree in business, finance or a law degree. Licenses such as the CPA

(Certified Public Accountant), CFA (Chartered Financial Analyst) or CFP (Certified Financial Planner), also helped to get one a better shot at an interview. Many firms also liked to hire people who were previous titans in industry or professional sports. The reasoning was in the hope that these former athletes, or those who had carved a strong reputation in the business world, could potentially bring in their former associates, players or contacts as possible clients. This would enable starting brokers to hit the ground running, bringing in assets that would generate commissions and additional revenues for the firm.

My resume was nothing to speak of; I didn't have the advantage of strong connections from previous employments to bring in as clients, and I wasn't a former professional athlete. I didn't know anyone personally who worked as a stockbroker, money manager or ran a firm, whether in accounting, brokerage or law. With these disadvantages, I knew I would have to get more industry-related experience and the licenses necessary to garner any interest from the firms I wanted to interview with eventually. My undergraduate degree had addressed the various complexities of money management on only a superficial level, not enough background to have any real applicable skills in the money management business.

While in the rehabilitation hospital, I had worked with a couple of occupational therapists who customized simple equipment to accommodate my particular limitations and injury. As I enjoyed reading, a plexiglass tray was designed to hook between my armrests, which could be used to hold books or magazines. For typing on a keyboard, I used a light aluminum mouth stick with a simple plastic insert to grip between my teeth, equipped with a rubber tip on one end for traction. This instrument also served to help me turn magazine and book pages. I even used the mouth stick to write this book, one letter or character at a time.

My reading material was now geared toward learning on a broad front, everything I could find on stocks and bonds, finance and geopolitical news. These pursuits would help contribute to my knowledge base and would also help significantly in a money management career. I read publications like *Forbes, Fortune, BusinessWeek, The Economist, Barron's* and *Investor's Daily*, as well as various newspapers like the *Wall Street Journal*.

After researching, I began to form a clearer vision of what potential firms were looking for among applicants and realized since I didn't have any connections, gaining some experience, licenses, and additional college level coursework, would hopefully give me a fighting chance. I would work to make potential employers feel at ease with my paralysis, not an easy task. The Vanguard Group was headquartered close by and I learned from a phone call I made to their main office, they were interviewing in their Marketing Department for phone representatives. If hired, I would be discussing the various mutual funds at Vanguard they offered with prospective and existing clients. They were also hiring for part-time, a perfect opportunity for me to gain some experience and a chance to work again. I knew I wasn't yet ready for full-time, wasn't even sure if my stamina could handle it.

My assistant coverage was not well established enough to have one assistant for at least eight hours straight, which full-time would require. After interviewing with Vanguard, they hired me for four hours a day, three days a week discussing mutual funds. I had to take several exams and be licensed to converse with clients on mutual funds, so this part-time position required that I obtain a Series 63 license. Vanguard covered the cost in-house, and I was even getting paid to take the exam. I was also able to arrange part-time hours that didn't require me to be there too early. That was good; it still took me awhile to get up in the morning, and I was still working to develop a more efficient and less time-consuming routine.

The position was a great experience; I was now in a large mutual fund company, learning about investments. Albeit, they were only mutual funds, but it was a good chance to get licensed and have industry-related work experience to add to my resume. It would also give me a better idea of what would be required to eventually go full-time and land a position with a brokerage firm. I knew my current system would require more testing, to eventually reach my goal of full-time employment.

After working part-time for Vanguard for about two months, I also started attending night school two nights a week taking classes, to gain more industry-specific knowledge. These courses were geared toward portfolio management, not only helpful in my career but would show on my resume that I was pursuing additional education. I had also hired competent assistants to assist me in the office and accompany me to night classes to take notes. These assistants were from local universities, and if possible, I would pick applicants who were majoring in studies that would compliment my new career. I also made sure they all had an active interest in what I was doing.

The benefit to both of us was mutual—they gained good hands-on work experience, and in the process, I had an assistant who took her position to new levels. They enjoyed what they were learning, and the majority of them were very responsible in the process. It was a win-win, enabling me to be more successful. I could now spend more time articulating fund differences and markets to clients while they took notes, listened in and kept things organized.

After working in the department for several more months, an opportunity to get a Series 7 license came up. I immediately jumped on the firm's offer; the Series 7 is required by the brokerage industry for a broker to be able to buy and sell a variety of investment products. By successfully acquiring this license, I knew that my marketability would be significantly increased. Any firm I applied to would also be aware I had passed an industry requirement to trade, had met SEC (Securities and Exchange Commission) regulations to do so, and had a strong working knowledge of investments. Fortunately, my other night classes had ended, freeing up the weeknights I needed to take the course. I signed up, and over the next eight weeks, two nights a week after work, an assistant would drive me to the class taking place at a college about an hour away.

At the completion of the class, the professor gave a practice exam to the roughly forty participants taking it, to give us an idea of how well we were prepared to sit for the federally mandated licensing exam. I studied hard for the exam, and when the results were tabulated, he announced that I had received the highest score in the class. I was elated. The passing of the proctored Series 7 licensing exam I took the following week was now behind me. I was now a licensed representative, eligible to trade in a variety of investment products from stocks and bonds, to options and other publicly traded offerings. I felt validated that the path I had chosen so many months earlier was one I could continue. The smaller goals I had set for myself had now all come together, and I was now ready to pursue my ultimate goal: interviewing for and hopefully landing a position with a large Wall Street firm.

Interviewing with Brokerage Firms

*"Faith is taking the first step even when you
don't see the whole staircase."*

—Dr. Martin Luther King Jr.

Continuing to work at Vanguard, I began exploring brokerage firms to see if they were hiring. Most had branch offices scattered around the suburbs, filled with mostly tenured money managers and were not in the habit of hiring new brokers. They wanted to recruit seasoned individuals who already had an established book of business. After some exploratory calls to local branches that became pretty clear. I then decided to set my sights on downtown Philadelphia, which was over an hour commute. Brokerage firms at the time didn't have much of a web presence, and no employment sites like Monster, Indeed or CareerBuilder existed to make applying easier. So I had to send all my applications and resumes by mail. Initial contact with these firms was by phone, usually getting a front office administrative assistant, who couldn't provide much detail on where the company stood on hiring, or for that matter, what the firm was looking for in an applicant. There was little to be gleaned from their sales brochure, with virtually no coverage on the myriad of questions I would have liked to have had answered in advance.

Typical conversations in exploratory calls to these firms were usually brief and ended with my requesting a packet and application to be mailed. Within the space of two weeks, I had about ten packages arrive in the mail. My assistant would open the envelopes and place the materials on the tray hooked to my electric chair. She would stand there patiently by my side, turning the pages of all this voluminous information. I would get a basic idea concerning that particular firm, though the information was pretty general. Talk about cumbersome, especially for my assistants helping me work through the stack.

Some of the larger firms I applied to who were national in scope; Merrill Lynch, Prudential, Dean Witter, to name a few. Other financial firms like Advest, Janney Montgomery Scott, and Wheat First Securities, had regional exposure on the East Coast, and all had big offices in Philadelphia. Most firms would only hire new brokers for their office if someone left or they had an opening at that location. I figured I would "blanket" Philadelphia with applications and see what stuck. New hires at some of the biggest and best of firms were offering very impressive starting salaries, some places carrying you for the first year up to eighteen months while you worked on building your client base. A few top firms also ran training programs. Whether internally or outsourced, they provided the new hire a chance to learn various sales techniques, about the firm's different product offerings, and an opportunity to become familiar with their unique computer systems and software. There was quite a lot to learn if I ever did get hired.

A few of the negatives of working in Philadelphia centered around the long commute and trying to find parking for my oversized van within a short distance. That eliminated most available outside lots downtown, and parking garages were impossible. The parking concerns were not yet an issue, similar to putting the cart before the horse. I didn't yet have an interview set up, or for that matter been offered a position. I knew though if I eventually was hired, that this was one of the many details that would have to be addressed and solved prior.

The hand-filled applications had now been completed and mailed out. Out of ten firms that sent applications, I ended up applying to seven. The other three didn't appeal to me for various reasons and the seven I applied to represented the biggest and best Philadelphia had to offer. I continued working at Vanguard, knowing it would probably be at least two to three weeks before I heard back from any, if at all.

One thing I had omitted in all the applications and cover letters was any mention of my paralysis. To some, this may seem a little misleading, leaving out my diminished physicality, though I didn't see it that way. The position I was interested in would require dedication, ambition, and ever-evolving knowledge. With an able assistant serving as my hands and mobile, I felt my personal limitations shouldn't be an issue. At least, that was how I saw things, and I would work very hard to portray that to the management who would grant interviews.

Hopefully, I could get potential employers to see beyond my chair, and that hard work combined with perseverance was more important than my perceived shortcomings. I wanted to make clear that my disability should be of no concern. I wanted them to see that my work history at Vanguard and licenses I had acquired supported this. My plan was that all firms would receive their application back from an aspiring applicant, who not only had industry experience but was also licensed. In their eyes, hopefully, my work experience and the licenses I had acquired meant they wouldn't have to carry me financially for the time I needed to study for the license, generally about three to four months. It wasn't unusual for a firm hiring a new broker to compensate them while they studied for the licensing exam. I felt my background would be pretty competitive with other applicants who didn't yet possess what I had obtained.

Roughly two weeks had passed when I received my first correspondence from one of the firms where I applied. My assistant opened the response letter and held it out for me to read. It was typed on company letterhead and was from one of the smaller regional firms where I applied. As I glanced down the letter, I noticed it read like a standard boilerplate rejection letter, *'I'm sorry to inform you, but we are not hiring at this time.'* I wasn't overly disappointed, it had not been the top firm I had applied to, and they did mention they would notify me if they were hiring in the future. What was a little annoying was that the office manager didn't even bother to sign the letter. It led me to wonder if it was an oversight, they didn't care, or worse; they had so many applicants that there wasn't time to sign each one by hand. The latter reason I knew was extreme, but I hoped it wasn't the case. If so, it would also lead one to think that perhaps all the other firms were besieged by hungry applicants like myself. All of us vying for the limited positions these companies may have available.

All of the firms were old and well-established, their downtown branches mostly mature offices, filled with many brokers, not start-ups, hungrily looking to fill empty spaces and cubicles with as many new faces as they could find. New hires were the exception at the firms I applied to and while more competitive, had limited positions available. They were all "real" financial institutions with strong roots and legitimate foundations. No applications were going to a boiler room operation with a "pump-and-dump" mentality. I steered clear from ones that I thought might only demand for credentials a slick delivery and a drifting moral compass, not wanting to be associated with that type of philosophy or firm. I wanted to work for a company with brand name recognition and one who was not only well respected in the industry but had withstood the test of time and the vagaries of market swoons over many painful periods. It would not only be easier to build a client base over time but as important; hopefully help ensure that the firm that hired me with these types of roots could survive a bad market like in 1929, 1973-74, 1987 and 2007-09. In the process, leaving their money managers unscathed in the aftermath.

Roughly another week went by, and a letter arrived from another regional firm where I applied. As the first two letters were from regional companies, I figured that possibly they were receiving the fewest applications or had a higher turnover. I reasoned, perhaps the huge multi-nationals were receiving the most applications and had a much lower broker turnover. Who knows? The largest firms were the most well known in the world, paid higher salaries, and had better benefits than their smaller counterparts. To be expected, it also meant much more competitive hiring practices. After my assistant had opened the letter, the wording was different than the first response I had received. They wanted to set up an interview—that was more like it! The first correspondence from a reputable regional firm that wanted to set up an interview.

I was batting .500 for interviews and was looking forward to the meeting and learning more about this firm. I planned on explaining how I could help them and try to assure them that my paralysis shouldn't be a factor. I would also share with them my office experience at Vanguard, assistant structure and why I had applied to them.

The interview was set up a week later, and I had arranged it on a day I wasn't working. I was looking forward to meeting the manager at this Philadelphia office. It was in the downtown financial district, and the office was in a large high-rise, taking up the entire 20th floor. I wasn't thrilled about being in a high-rise, especially being in a wheelchair. If the power went out, rendering the elevators useless, if there were a fire, on to a host of other possibilities, it would be tough for me to get out. I didn't let that influence my decision to interview, though. I had already learned that all the big brokerage firms downtown were in high-rises, none on any floors lower than the fifth. I had allowed about an hour and a half for traffic and parking, so we arrived comfortably at the elevator banks inside the building's lobby with about fifteen minutes to spare. My assistant pushed the button for the twentieth floor. We both rode up in silence. I was quiet, not nervous, just mentally gearing myself up.

This was my second interview since my accident, and I figured it would be much more challenging than my first one at Vanguard.

Vanguard was known to hire part-time seasonal workers during busy periods, unlike brokerage firms, so it had made my prospects of getting hired there much easier. I felt prepared, though my work experience was pretty weak. Before my accident, I found employment with a Fortune 50, multi-national oil company, though it had only lasted three weeks before I was hurt. I had been employed at Vanguard for only six months on a part-time basis.

My tenure at these companies was extremely light, to say the least. My background, albeit not long in work history, at least included on my resume the broker's licenses required to trade and the fact I was employed in a somewhat similar industry. I'm pretty sure that's what landed the interview, now it was up to me to get this firm to see the big picture and look beyond my injury. Since the accident, I had learned much about myself. The operations and procedures I endured in the hospital and afterward were quite demanding, making this interview in my mind, child's play in comparison. I wasn't nervous or had any fear going in, more a determination and drive to continue forward and realize my goal.

The elevator doors opened, and a beautiful lobby greeted us, replete with what appeared to be expensive furniture and décor. An equally attractive secretary was behind the front desk, busy talking on the phone, her other hand typing furiously on the keyboard in front of her monitor. She glanced up and smiled, motioning with one spare finger that she would be available in a moment as I wheeled closer. She hung up, typed a little more and asked whom we were there to meet. On the surface, it wouldn't have been hard for her to think I was a client meeting his money manager and not showing up for an interview. As mentioned, I didn't make any reference on my resume or cover letter regarding my disability, so she had no idea why I was there. I resolved her query quickly by providing my name and introduced her to my assistant. She then called the interviewing manager to let him know I had arrived for our one o'clock interview. About ten minutes later, he walked in and immediately extended his hand for me to shake. I laughed and said,

"I let my assistant shake the hands." My assistant reached out, and he shook her hand. He didn't appear to be uncomfortable although he did seem a little taken back by my wheelchair, I thought.

I'm sure, never in his wildest dreams, did he visualize my resume and background attached to a guy who motored his electric wheelchair by puffing or sipping from a straw connected to a gooseneck. I had already noticed months earlier, not only at Vanguard but out in public as well, that people I encountered had no idea how I was able to move the chair. I also knew they didn't have any idea what I was doing with that straw I kept putting in my mouth. Was I drinking something, or getting oxygen out of that tube?

I realized soon after I was discharged from the rehabilitation center and was back home, this question among many others, most likely swirled around in the minds of most people who made my acquaintance for the first time or weren't familiar with my chair's technology. Early on, I decided that the right thing to do was to take the initiative and explain how my electric chair is controlled. I put myself in their shoes, seeing the wonderment and questions in their eyes, many revolving around the technology as they looked at me. I also realized it would help put new people I encountered at ease. By explaining the mechanics of the chair and what purpose the straw served, I would accomplish other objectives as well.

For those unfamiliar with my situation, after explaining, it would allow the dialogue to move forward to things I was interested in discussing. By letting them know I was not relying on the straw for health reasons, and that I was even healthier than what I tried to portray by smiling and sitting straight. I learned this was important to convey early on. Not only to prospective employers and new people I would meet, but also those interviewing for assistant positions.

By letting potential employers know upfront about my chair's mechanics and that I was in good health, could hopefully provide some assurance I could be considered a reliable employee who would work hard to get to the office and not call out for medical reasons.

Explaining the chair up front to new applying assistants would also help them to realize that I was an easy person to care for, and they shouldn't have any worries. Most important for both groups was that they didn't see my disability as an issue, whether hiring me or working for me. It would hopefully clarify and satisfy to some degree, potential worries in both camps around my chair and health. Going forward, I would also work to solidify that position, hopefully building their trust in the process.

To also garner more buy-in from future employers throughout my work history, it was important that I have a very sharp and capable assistant accompany me to work. Other pertinent factors I required in an office assistant ranged from appropriate dress for an office environment to some working knowledge in my field, mostly gleaned from their college courses. The helpful traits these assistants possessed would go a long way, not only in my career but also in public. Employers being aware that I was well cared for would help eliminate concern on their part, in case some emergency came up while in the office.

I knew in advance that shyness or insecurity were not traits that would take you far in the money management business. My assistants learned early on when meeting employers or co-workers to not only be personable but also try to make eye contact and extend their hand to shake for me, hopefully before the other person did it first. It would also help to solidify in future employers' minds that we were a well-established and coordinated team. It was important that the interviewer, future managers, and clients see us as two working together with strong, seamless interactions as opposed to one who is broken physically assisted by another. I worked to create the image in interviewers' minds that they were hiring a well-oiled personable machine, one with two brains, twice the creativity, each with drive and ready to move forward with ambition and goals. Plus, if hired, they were only responsible for one salary. By accomplishing all the above in a very short period of time, the employer, or in this case, the office manager, would feel more comfortable with me going into the interview. In their mind,

I'm sure many questions remained. I planned on chipping away at those as we proceeded.

The office manager led the way for my assistant and me to an empty conference room for what I thought was our interview. I was informed that I first had to complete a 200 question psychological exam. Well, that was a new one. I didn't expect it going in, and had never taken one before. I was informed it was firm policy. I presumed they probably hired a couple of stockbrokers who didn't work out and thought by checking under all applicants' mental hoods, it might help minimize hiring mistakes. For whatever reason, they considered the test necessary.

My assistant filled in the little circles while I provided her the answers. About fifty questions in, I noticed the questions were starting to get weird, some very strange, at least in my mind. One question was, *'Would you rather see your father whipped or a horse?'* Well, neither was a choice in my mind, but I had to choose one or the other. It wasn't tough to answer since I love my father deeply. Some poor, imaginary horse in their question had to be the scapegoat. Later on, probably fifty or more questions in, they began to ask similar questions to the whipping question. Maybe, the psychologist(s) writing the questions thought that by placing similar ones an hour or so into the test, my mind might have changed. Perhaps, somewhere deep in the subconscious recesses of my mind, I was still troubled by the treatment of that poor horse and would change my answer. Didn't change in my case, but prospective interviewees with average to poor father relationships might have sided with the horse.

I stuck with the poor horse getting whipped, but could imagine others taking the test, shaking their head like me, thinking, *'what the…?'* Who knows? About as silly a question to me, as, *'would you rather see a sibling tortured or a bunny rabbit?'* Just to clear the air, I don't advocate whipping or abuse in any form, whether my family, other humans or animals. These questions I presume were somehow geared to uncover inconsistencies and weed out those with perceived abnormal behavior.

Two hours later, my mind tired from some pretty bizarre questions, I was ready to move on. Now that the test was complete, hopefully, I would have an opportunity to discuss with the manager of the firm, what they were looking for and my work experience.

Though it was their company policy to administer such a test for new applicants, I wasn't convinced that such a test of this nature could uncover whether a person would be an honest broker, let alone a good revenue generator for the firm. The questions were all over the board, making one almost feel they had stepped into Alice in Wonderland and were being grilled by the Mad Hatter.

I felt like I was sitting in the empty chair listening and responding at the Mad Hatter's tea party.

I had my assistant take the completed psychology test to the front desk per the office manager's instructions, and the front desk secretary let him know I was finished. He came back into the lobby, thanked me, and informed me if I passed the psychology test, a second interview would be set up, and we could proceed from there.

His words took me a little by surprise. It certainly wasn't what I expected after completing the test—driving all the way to Center City, Philadelphia to what I thought was an interview. The interview letter made no mention of a prior psychology test. In hindsight, I was a little surprised this firm drew the line at the test and didn't at least have me interview to some degree. No other company I had ever worked for through the years ever used one. The firm could have possibly been burned by some bad types they had hired that came to light after one of many market meltdowns throughout history. In the annals of time, there have always been unscrupulous people, sadly costing smaller investors anywhere from their life-savings to large investors losing multiple millions. I wasn't sure how some of their questions would expose that, but I'm not a trained psychologist either.

A letter arrived from the firm a week or so later, saying I didn't pass the psychological test. Well, immediately after opening the letter and seeing the rejection, I didn't get upset. I also didn't expect anyone to show up in a van with a patch above their coat pocket with a soothing name like Pleasant Meadows emblazoned across a field of wildflowers on a white garment, forcing me to take a ride to their facility. I was just surprised that's where it ended. To not pass didn't bother me greatly, I was just more curious than anything else what *"flagged me."* I just shook my head and laughed. Either I didn't pass as they claimed, or maybe it was just a ploy not to take the interview further. Impossible to know, either way, even my surprise entry may have been troubling.

I never saw the results or what questions thwarted my interviewing further. As a side note, regardless of getting that job, I would never throw my father under the bus for any reason. Incidentally, he was glad to know that when I shared the question. We both got a laugh over it and to this day I still have reservations about these tests, but I understand more employers are using them in their hiring practice. So, for those reading this and facing one with a company you're applying to, good luck!

I continued working at Vanguard, gaining more experience in investments and working with clients, often covering a myriad of questions they would pose concerning their accounts. Some questions were straightforward; discussing Vanguard funds, and covering anything from the fund's philosophy, management, performance as well as the stocks or bonds they held. Other questions were more complex, ranging from geopolitics, the economy, and the potential impact (positive or negative) on a fund's performance if certain economic events or variables unfolded.

I shared with clients that the vagaries of the market were tough to forecast. Most importantly, each client's individual needs were the priority, as one would expect. I would provide them with historical perspectives, like a rise or fall in interest rates, the impact of trade tariffs, politics, regulations, war, and other things that could have an influence on their portfolio. Not only how extraneous events could affect a specific fund, but also the ramifications to their overall asset mix. There are always many broad-based possibilities or events brewing simultaneously around the globe, demanding due diligence on my part, requiring me to keep abreast on many fronts. This level of responsibility weighed heavily as it should and required constant monitoring.

Over the next two weeks, I received two other letters in the mail, one from a fairly large regional firm that wanted to set up an interview, and another from a large national firm that wasn't hiring at the moment. I was happy to get another interview, though my enthusiasm was a little muted concerning the rejection letter by the larger firm. At this point, I had received four replies back to the seven applications that I had sent out. Overall, I was impressed with the response time, as it was through the mail.

I was still batting .500 on getting interviews, though I wasn't yet on base. I was hoping the next interview would be more productive, and that I might have a chance to go over my resume and qualifications. I wanted the opportunity to share with the manager how I planned to bring in clients and how my injury wouldn't affect my performance.

Also, I wanted to explain how I had adapted to my physical limitations to succeed in my current role at Vanguard, utilizing a well-trained assistant to help me. The week flew by quickly. I looked forward to the following interview, and the possibility of becoming a practicing money manager.

The next Tuesday, my assistant and I headed toward Philadelphia. It was about eighty-five degrees, sunny, with a gentle breeze, basically, perfect weather and the drive was uneventful. The interview was at 1 pm, and we made it to an outdoor lot to park, only about three blocks away from the firm's high-rise, their building situated about three blocks from City Hall on Market Street. I was feeling good, not nervous, just going with the flow. My assistant and I proceeded down Market Street toward their building. After we had made it about a block, I glanced down, and much to my consternation noticed the front of my slacks was wet!

I knew we hadn't spilled anything and I quickly realized that the catheter must have come undone and in the process, leaked onto my pants. I called over to my assistant and explained what happened, though it was pretty darn obvious when she saw my head nod downward. We ducked between two buildings, away from foot traffic, and waited for an opportunity to see what had happened. She remedied the situation, though unfortunately, by this time my pants were already noticeably wet and there were only about twenty minutes left until the interview.

Thoughts raced through my head, ranging from '*Why the heck did this have to happen now!?*' to quickly, '*What should I do, call and reschedule?*' I came to a fast decision; as it was sunny, a little breezy and warm, I thought if I sat facing the sun for the remaining fifteen minutes, maybe, just maybe they would dry enough not to be noticeable. I shared my thoughts with my assistant and that we would give it a try. We had come this far, and I didn't want to call at the last minute and cancel. I wasn't sure if they would set up another interview and I didn't want to chance it. So, I sat there, the bright sun shining down on me, and fortunately, the decent breeze seemed to be having positive results. After about ten minutes, the pants were starting to dry on top, a good sign.

Five minutes later, only a faint outline remained, some of the mild dampness now obscured by the dark fabric. There were about five minutes left till the interview as we continued toward the building, still in the sun, its rays not yet hidden by the tall buildings that surrounded us. As we arrived, I kept glancing down at my watch, knowing I would stay outside until the last minute, trying to allow any telltale traces to evaporate away. This wasn't the first time I had experienced something like this, fortunately, a rare occurrence, just the first time going to an interview. Thankfully, these mishaps are few and far between.

I knew in past experiences like this, obviously the best scenario if possible, was to change my pants, wash off, clean the cushion and continue with my day. That luxury was impossible now. I was a minute away from my interview time and in the middle of downtown Philadelphia. I glanced down again, now only a very faint, barely visible outline remained. I told my assistant we were going in, this was a mission that couldn't be further delayed. She affirmed the pants were looking better, and knew how I felt about not continuing through with what we both had set out to do. I've had plenty of other disappointments and unexpected situations with this injury, many times before this incident. Over time, I worked hard to rid my mind of negativity and helplessness and try to replace those feelings with a dogged determination to look beyond the issue and try to find a solution. In my case and excuse the pun, come hell or high water, I wasn't going to be denied this chance to interview—too many things were already in motion.

We went into the building, and my assistant pushed the elevator button for the fifth floor where the firm's office was located. They occupied the entire floor much like the brokerage where I had previously interviewed. Hopefully, this firm wouldn't whip out another psychological test. I didn't want to have my merits or abilities judged by faceless questions, where I would never have the opportunity to interact with those presenting the test or interviewing me.

We arrived at the fifth floor; the elevator doors opened onto another beautiful foyer. It was as spectacular as the lobby in my first interview.

I wheeled up to the desk, sneaking a glance down at my pants, to see if their artificial lighting would highlight the predicament I had found myself in. Thankfully it didn't, though I did notice a slight odor of urine, something not as prevalent outdoors, where more wind and open air made it barely perceptible. Well, it seemed noticeable to me now, and I thought that hopefully, the interviewing manager wouldn't be sitting too close. While waiting for them to come out, I envisioned that we would be separated by a large conference table, they on one side and me on the other. Or something of the sort, putting some distance between us. The receptionist smiled and said the manager would be right out. My assistant sat down in a chair as I parked mine next to her. At least she and others in the lobby didn't move to other seats away from me!

I asked her to rummage around in my backpack to see if I had any deodorant or cologne inside. I never carried those items usually, but you never know what an assistant will leave in there until it's cleaned out. Hopefully, she would locate something to camouflage the obvious smell to some degree. I wouldn't have hesitated to have liberally showered myself with anything pleasing if available, in the hopes that perhaps it would help mask the smell somewhat. Maybe I would have come off as an overeager, well-dowsed interviewee as opposed to one who may not be cognizant that his pants were wet, or his hygiene routine was suspect.

Either way, this was a heck of a predicament. Surprisingly, I wasn't that worked up or upset, just more annoyed that it had happened. I wasn't that nervous about interviewing either, feeling I had a fairly strong resume now and was employed by one of their bigger competitors. I felt that my interview was similar to recruiting a minor player for their team who had good prospects. At least, that's how I saw it. A couple of minutes later someone who I assumed was the manager hurried out. After introducing himself, he took the file handed to him and motioned me to follow him down the hall. I had already introduced my assistant as he shook her hand. I asked her to wait in the lobby, as I followed him down a narrow hall past a few doors.

The next thing I knew, he was opening a door leading into what appeared to be a small room. He flipped the light switch, confirming my suspicions. Wow, what a big disappointment. The manager went into the room to move the table, to accommodate my wheelchair, that's how small it was. He shoved it over against one wall and then had to wheel two of the three chairs around the table out into the hall. This room was obviously meant for a very small meeting, three or four people tops. It appeared to be designed for a stockbroker/money manager and his client who came in, as it looked like there were many other rooms down the hall designed for a similar purpose.

I glanced down one more time as he shut the door, his back facing me. Fortunately, the stain was no longer noticeable. The smell, though, at least to me, was another story. I wasn't yet sure what his thoughts were concerning the prevalent odor. Now, I wasn't known for a keen sense of smell, probably about average, so unless I was lucky and this guy couldn't smell at all, maybe having anosmia, chances are he would notice. Sadly, about five million people in this country are affected by anosmia, commonly known as "nose blindness," where their sense of smell is virtually nonexistent. It was a long shot; with roughly 325 million people living in the United States, the odds were only about one in sixty-five in my favor.

I took for granted he could smell, and winced a little as he shut the door. Two bodies now squeezed in an eight by eight-foot office. I glanced around, noticing there were no visible signs of a ventilation system either, much to my chagrin. Never in one's imagination could someone come up with something so tragically comical, and this was taking place in real time.

As he was going over my resume, I was thinking to myself that this scenario reminded me of the writing of the old Seinfeld series, spawned by the creative and funny genius of Larry David and Jerry Seinfeld. An episode, centered around a paralyzed guy who had worked hard, accomplishing a series of goals to get a shot at an interview with a brokerage firm, whose pants accidentally became wet at the last moment. I almost felt like Kramer or George. Finding myself trapped in a cramped, non-ventilated room interviewing for a job, thinking I had a one in sixty-five shot the guy wouldn't notice!

The interview proceeded along as he asked questions geared around my resume and work experience. I elaborated on my position at Vanguard, emphasizing what I knew about the brokerage business, on to answering a variety of other financial questions he posed. I explained my chair mechanics, and how I rely on an accomplished assistant to help me during the day and what minimal and inexpensive office configurations I required with my limitations. This led to other questions about how I would be able to interact with clients, my office equipment needs and so on. I answered each one, providing a lot of detail and various examples as the interview proceeded.

At this stage, the smell in the room seemed much more noticeable than before, and with only two people in the room, I was pretty sure he knew who it was with the issue. Amazingly, and believe me I looked for signs, he didn't show any distress or project an image that something was amiss. We continued to talk for about an hour, and I even wondered if I should mention something like *"Hey, I had a freak thing happen, very unusual—my pants aren't generally wet, but today they are—did you notice?"* or, *"By the way, I smell something, is this room ok?"* Upon contemplation, I knew that there wasn't a suitable way to bring up the issue. It was a little too embarrassing, and for a first interview, I felt a real killer to my chances of a job offer, let alone a second interview.

My second thought to ask him if the room was "okay," didn't have much appeal either. I speculated it would most likely lead to the offer of a room change, where the same smell would accompany us into the new space, like a well-trained hunting dog that is hard to shake. Either way, the interview was over, and the manager had worked his way through all his questions. Some were complex, others just broad and only a few specific to my needs. He never showed any discomfort or signs he wanted to end the interview early.

In looking at the interview objectively, I thought it went well considering the situation, as bizarre as it was. It was also comforting that when he opened the door he didn't loosen his tie and stagger down the hall, gasping for breath. As I followed him back down the corridor, I couldn't fault him if he did, or at the very least, take in large gulps of fresh air.

Upon entering the lobby, he smiled, and I sensed a genuine person here, a compassionate person overall, and not about to embarrass someone at his firm with a disability. That, or he was one heck of an actor, a good poker player or had anosmia. Either way, he said he would let me know. He had a few other candidates that he was going to interview and remarked that he appreciated the time spent. I thanked him in turn, and my assistant reached out to shake his hand for me again, look him in the eyes and smile: customary protocol.

Previously mentioned in other areas in this book, I always found it made for a less awkward situation for those we encountered, if I had my assistant react first when shaking hands if possible. I learned it looked more seamless and less awkward for the interviewer, manager or person I had never met when I couldn't shake theirs back. By doing so, it would also lessen the concern on their part that they had committed some horrible disability gaffe or error. Kind of amusing to me, was if they were too fast on the draw, or at times I was out alone, when people extended their hand and noticing that I couldn't shake theirs, would often keep the gesture going by patting the top of my hand at that stage, usually about two or more times.

I would assure them it was no big deal, smiling as we moved on to other topics. Sad was when I first arrived home, and the family dog ran up to greet me after I had been away for so long, wanting to be patted. Sam would notice I couldn't (or wouldn't) pet her, but she would still try, sticking her nose and muzzle under my fingers and palm trying to receive those pats. Animals, as we know are smart, she gave up very shortly after that perhaps sensing that I was unable and that it wasn't due to the fact I didn't want to. Over time, as my assistants learned to take the initiative when shaking hands, they were usually first and successful in the greeting. Especially, if the other party didn't have lightning fast "Wild Bill" Hickok skills!

While boarding the elevator, the doors shutting behind us, I couldn't help but wonder; did the interviewing manager possibly against all odds have anosmia? To ask him would have been too obvious, but he sure hid his discomfort well if he didn't.

The next week went by smoothly. I continued my classes at night and spent four days a week at Vanguard working with clients. I had increased my daily hours as well, now putting in six hours, wanting to ramp up my day to be longer. A position with a brokerage firm would be more than forty hours a week, so I knew I had to gradually lengthen the time I spent working and learn some things about my stamina in the process. By upping my hours and the number of days per week that I worked, I realized early on that my assistants preferred the longer days. It was more money for them. For me, it proved that I could balance a demanding work schedule with my physical limitations. I didn't mind seeing my paycheck go up as well, affording me an opportunity to save more, pay bills and have more funds available for things I wanted or needed.

A letter arrived the following week from the firm where I had interviewed. Bearing news that didn't surprise me. They wrote that they appreciated my time and would keep my application on file, but had chosen another candidate. I presume the one they chose mostly likely didn't have wet pants right before they interviewed. I made a decision that I wouldn't try to second-guess myself, preferring instead to learn from the experience and move on.

One can always wonder if I should have just canceled at the last minute due to my unforeseen mishap and try to reschedule. Knowing how competitive the industry was in Philadelphia, and what was involved for me to arrange and get there, superseded any thoughts about not going forward. Of course, if they didn't dry so well outside, or I thought the smell was more noticeable early on, of course, I would have reconsidered and canceled.

Though I didn't get hired, it was still a good experience; my first candid and intense interview with a large regional financial firm. I had learned some things. Now I had an opportunity to fine-tune what was discussed at the interview. After leaving, I thought back and recalled a few questions I knew I could tighten my answers to and present stronger replies in future interviews. As the interview was fairly in-depth, I appreciated the opportunity and knew I would be better prepared when the next one came around.

Though unforeseen, my incident also prompted me to be more prepared going forward. This did not equate to me loading my van with cases of Axe, eight pairs of pants, and a variety of colognes, just that I employed a better checklist going forward. No different from a pilot before he heads out into the wild blue yonder. Going forward, I paid more attention to not only medical mishap possibilities, but I also made sure my electric chair was properly charged, among other things. I assure you, pushing my chair with me aboard to get recharged is not easy. Preparing myself, for about any circumstance, I learned is a good idea. As a result, over the following years, depending on the issue, it was possible to mitigate or at least minimize what could have turned out to be a challenging day, much like that interview.

At this time I had received four letters back from applications, two were rejection letters and two interviews that didn't pan out. Three other applications were still outstanding, one with another regional and two with large, multi-national firms. A week later, I received a letter from one of the large multi-national companies. To me, it was the most important application out of the seven I had mailed. The one firm out of the seven where I applied, that I hoped would show interest. They too, like the others, were in a high-rise. I opened the letter, and my heart skipped a beat, it was from Merrill Lynch, and they wanted to interview me! I couldn't believe it; the top firm in Philadelphia wanted to get together.

Merrill Lynch was one of the quintessential firms at the time, before the 2007-2009 market meltdown, after which they were absorbed into Bank of America. The company also boasted the most recognized and famous logo on the street; a stampeding bull and all that it symbolized. To make it even more surreal, their flagship branch in Philadelphia wanted to interview me. A location that was one block from Philadelphia's City Hall, occupying the entire top floor of the high-rise they were in, thirty-five stories up. It was situated in some of the most expensive office rental space in the whole city. I was elated. My top brokerage firm choice and they wanted to interview me. It was all I could do not to show the letter to everyone I knew.

Though it was only an interview letter, to me it was so much more. It provided me the validation that the goals and steps I had taken to move forward after my injury, were now starting to come together. Not just a dream anymore or an unknown destination on the far side of a map. I knew I needed to shine at this interview; it was down to the last three I had applied to.

It was my third interview out of seven applications I had mailed, and the fifth response I had received back. Difficult to imagine that kind of interview success ratio, but I chalked it up to four things; licenses I had acquired, the firm I was employed by, additional course work I had completed geared toward the position I was seeking, and luck. Some may think, and I can include myself looking back, perhaps some divine intervention was added to the mix. Who knows? Luck is hard to quantify, and I believe that three of the four reasons I even got an interview, were due to goals I had worked hard to accomplish. I believe they were critical to getting noticed in this industry.

Another reason the interview was such a surprise was the length of time that had passed since I mailed the application to Merrill Lynch. The last two firms that had received applications from me hadn't even responded yet, so I had no idea where they stood. I tried not to think about it too much, and though I felt ready, I was somewhat nervous. I realized there was quite a bit at stake riding on this interview.

I knew it was important to be well prepared for Merrill. The firm was a leader in its industry and had many former professional athletes knocking on its door for employment, as well as former chief executives and senior officers of companies who were interested in switching careers. The athletes; hired after their prowess on the field had waned, and were looking to bring in some of their former athlete friends or wealthy fans that admired them on the gridiron to invest. The firms also sought out executives to hire, normally after they had left their mark on the corporate world, going after all the connections they may have made throughout their career. If having left on good terms with the corporations they were with, perhaps investing employee rollovers at retirement and other investing needs. If big enough in the company, perhaps working with corporate cash, placing in short-term bond instruments for them or bringing in investment banking deals, whether merger related, subsidiary spin-offs or for other investment banking reasons.

So my lack of connections combined with other reasons made my interview with Merrill a bit of a surprise. My name wasn't famous, I wasn't a former professional athlete and had never been head of a company in a previous career, let alone ever held a significant position. A Series 63 and Series 7 broker's license, less than a year of industry experience at Vanguard, coupled with a Bachelor of Science in Economics and some extra finance and portfolio management classes I completed in night school after work were all that my resume showed. But somehow, some way, it was enough. Perhaps Lady Luck and the Divine were smiling on me much more than I realized.

At this stage, though I wasn't looking back, never feeling intimidated by what I lacked, whether on my resume or physically. I had already been through so much and survived multiple challenges up to this point. Discovering more about myself in the process, new strengths which would help me going forward. I was also still hungry to keep going, not yet satisfied with where I was in my life. I hadn't spent any real time in the corporate world and was a far cry from being anywhere near financially independent. I knew there were many more things I wanted to find out about myself and what was possible. This interview was just one more hurdle and step on my journey. If the interview went well, terrific and if not, I would continue approaching other firms while still working at Vanguard.

I had gathered through basic research that this was a well-established office that had been in Philadelphia since 1940, in various locations in the city. They were the largest brokerage firm in the world, formed in 1915 in New York City under its current name, Merrill Lynch, through the merger of several different firms going back to 1872 with Cassatt and Company. It was an old moneyed firm with a lot of clout, having hired sharp and innovative employees throughout their history. Some of their staff had introduced many breakthroughs in the industry early on, way ahead of others.

For instance, they were the first firm to use computers to log and track orders, the first to introduce a Cash Management Account (CMA), which is basically a cash managed account that you could write checks from and where trades would settle, sort of a savings and checking account combined. Merrill was also the first to use wire services, virtual pioneers of the financial world in so many ways.

The following Friday rolled around, interview day. The assistant going along was as ready as I, dressed professionally and excited like me. She had been with me at Vanguard, and we had grown to know each other, making our appearance in front of others one of smooth teamwork. Her ability, as well as others I would employ and train through the years to anticipate my needs or cues almost appeared telepathic at times; the signals were so subtle. From my giving a slight head movement at the screen on a particular computer program, to mouthing words silently to her while on the phone with a client to get needed material, was sometimes all it would take. I knew my assistant, and I had to present well as a team at the interview with Merrill.

I was applying for a coveted position with a top firm hopefully offering me a career on Wall Street, so everything had to be well thought out in advance. Sloppiness, a lack of attention to detail and poor preparation, meant you were probably trying to work for the wrong firm.

Maybe those shortcomings would play well in a "bucket shop" or dealing with penny stocks, but not with wealthy, successful types you wanted as clients. These types of investors took preparation, sharpness and good ideas for granted, much like breathing clean mountain air and it better stay fresh. I knew that everything from my appearance, thoughtful insights and strong, original responses to the manager's questions was paramount to having any success in this interview.

I arrived about twenty minutes early with no mishaps or issues, not that I expected any, but you never know. After we had entered the building, I mentioned to the security guard that we had a meeting with Merrill Lynch. I had been in few buildings this tall downtown, and the thought of possibly working on a thirty-fifth floor was a little intimidating going in, though I worked to override that. Heights had never bothered me, but in a wheelchair, it could be a problem for many reasons. I had limited knowledge at the time of high-rise tragedies. Though I was well aware that throughout the course of America's long history, the majority of most major cities had experienced significant disasters from fires to earthquakes, and the resultant damage to buildings or infrastructure was usually devastating.

We exited the elevator on their floor, my eyes taking in a massive open floor plan filled with cubicles, the outer walls lined with what appeared to be private offices. All of the offices had glass walls and glass doors, filled with what seemed to be seasoned brokers. Many were on the phone, some standing with headsets on looking out their window talking or if facing us, their computer screen. Others were not on the phone, just staring at the ticker tape display as it scrolled across one wall. A few took notice of my assistant and me as we waited by the elevator, as there was no lobby.

I found myself glancing up at the ticker tape display as well; a huge, long electronic strip with the lit up symbols of companies that had last traded flying by, followed by their final trade price. Bringing my focus back to the room, I noticed the majority of cubicles were full. The empty ones seemed to be just brokers out of the office as they also had computers, pictures and other things in the space. I watched some of the brokers standing and typing on their keyboard at the same time, *probably getting stock quotes, client or company information*, I thought.

An older woman approached my assistant and me looking poised, her steel gray hair neatly done. She shared with us that she was the office manager's personal assistant, and came across as professional, no nonsense and smart. She also projected an air of cultivated wisdom that appeared to be the product of years working in the financial district. She motioned us to follow her to the end of the floor toward what was obviously the largest glass-walled office on this penthouse floor, taking up an enormous corner. I wheeled to where she motioned my assistant and me to wait, noticing a man of about fifty inside on the phone. He was talking with his back facing us looking out his glass office walls, standing in front of what had to be a seven or eight-foot-long ornate desk made out of what looked like cherry, complete with matching cabinets. The cabinet tops were covered with what appeared to be expensive glassware, adorned with quite a few trophies, some of them fairly large. I thought they were positioned with care and thought on their surfaces.

I noticed all of his office exterior walls were also glass, from floor to ceiling and looked out over the city. The view out of one of the glass walls on the far side of his office and only one city block away was the statue of William Penn standing at eye level with us on top of Philadelphia's City Hall. The other outside walls also presented a breathtaking panorama as well. Quite an office I thought, wondering how many days and months it would take not to admire this incredible view for hours and get work accomplished.

Market Street in downtown Center City Philadelphia,
facing City Hall. Merrill's building is on the left.

At about the same moment, I felt the buzz of energy on the entire floor from all the brokers talking, phones ringing and orders being hurriedly rushed to a room near where I was sitting with brass bars on the front. Brokers who were walking by me at a fast pace who had just landed a trade and were delivering their order tickets to one of two busy assistants typing the orders handed to them, into their terminals. Orders once entered, that were then given to Merrill's floor clerks on the floor of the New York Stock or American Stock Exchange. These clerks would then rush them to the various specialists posts that dealt in the shares of the public companies that Merrill's clients, large and small, were looking to buy or sell.

I felt a little more nervous at this stage, having never experienced a large brokerage firm with swarming brokers hurriedly going back and forth from their desks, participating in a busy trading day. Besides my two interviews with the brokerage companies that had turned me down, my exposure to a firm with significant clout on Wall Street was non-existent. Prior visuals or exposure for me was limited mainly to some old stock footage, inserted in short films on the history of the exchanges while in several business classes in school. Of course, I had seen a few iconic movies like *Wall Street* with Charlie Sheen and Michael Douglas portraying their version of Wall Street, as well as various documentaries on the Crash of 1929.

Some butterflies were now starting to move around in my stomach as it dawned on me what this interview represented. All my dreams, planning and steps to get to this point, the goals I had established and worked toward, the many ups and downs, had come to fruition. Right here and now, in front of this glass door. I steeled myself and caught my breath as the manager hung up the phone and came to his door. He beckoned us to enter his office as my assistant stood next to me while I introduced her. She held out her hand as he was starting to extend his, saving him the uncertainty of whose hand he would be shaking. I laughed, thinking it sounded a little weak at the time and remarked, "I let her shake hands."

He laughed politely as I followed him into his beautiful, expansive office. I asked my assistant to wait outside. His personal assistant, whom we had met earlier, came in and handed him a folder. He opened the folder not saying a word, only reading what was contained within. As he perused the pages in the folder, I couldn't help but look out on the panoramic view laid out in front of me.

Looking out his office walls, I noticed all the major bridges feeding in and out of Philadelphia, not surprisingly, filled with busy traffic. We were up over 470 feet in the air, and at the time, it felt high to me, though that is somewhat small for tall buildings by today's standards. The cars appeared as miniature toys, going across little bridges. The helicopters out in the distance looked like gnats or mosquitoes flying across the greenish Delaware River far below, its water moving with tankers and barges. The view was breathtaking, and as one can imagine, there was so much activity and life moving about below.

I pulled myself back a little mentally, bringing my focus back into the room. Trying hard to gauge this man standing in front of me, the one who held my dreams and hopes in his hands. He had mentioned at the door his name was Mike Boland and to call him Mike. He ran not only the Center City office for Merrill Lynch, but also their Independence Square office, the two most successful and profitable locations in the entire financial district in all of the Philadelphia area. At the time, this was *the firm* in Philadelphia and still is: big, powerful and easily dwarfing all the other brokerage firms for prestige, clout, assets and generating revenue. I found out later Mike happened to be good friends with William Smith as well, the grandson of one of the original founders of Merrill Lynch, Pierce, Fenner, and Smith.

I realized as he flipped through the folder, I had a lot to lose if this interview didn't go well, but knew I had come a long way since the accident. I was sitting in the manager's office of the top firm in Philadelphia, waiting for him to proceed. As I sat there, the nervousness I felt initially started ebbing away, being replaced by stronger feelings of confidence. Perhaps I was feeding off all the energy that permeated this busy penthouse floor, or maybe it was from being more self-aware after coming through so much. I had no idea why I felt more relaxed but knew I wanted a chance to work here.

Though my experience was limited, I had learned a lot in the preceding year while at Vanguard. Suddenly, my self-reflections were interrupted as he remarked, "Well, I see something on this resume I like."

That was it, no explanation of what, until he said, *"Your birthday."* That threw me for a moment, then it dawned on me, Mike must have been born on the same day I was. Those odds at three hundred and sixty-five to one were an even longer shot than the previous interview where I hoped the interviewing manager had anosmia, at sixty-five to one. This time, the even longer odds had worked in my favor, though that point was mostly irrelevant when considering the position I was seeking, nothing much beyond a freak coincidence.

I laughed and remarked, "That's great, I have enjoyed that day too!" That broke the ice and right then; I sensed he was a nice guy with a good sense of humor.

We began discussing other things on my resume. He noticed the license requirements were out of the way, though he didn't comment whether or not that was a big deal to the firm. He proceeded to ask me about Vanguard, how I was able to interact with clients and how I made phone calls. I explained that my assistant he had met earlier sat next to me, both of us sharing the computer screen and how we each wore headphones wired to the same phone. I mentioned, "She dials the numbers; I talk, and she listens in, taking notes and filling out order tickets in the process." I also added that I didn't require any significant changes to a desk and computer arrangement, just two headphones connected to the same line.

He seemed okay with my response. He didn't provide any feedback to my answer, either way, mulling it over in his head. I discussed my college background, additional course work I was taking, and most importantly, why I wanted to work with Merrill Lynch and what I knew about the firm. Everything seemed to flow at least to me, who knows what he was thinking. I'm sure he had a lot on his plate running two of the biggest locations domestically for Merrill Lynch outside of New York City, and it appeared to be a busy trading day.

He began to wrap up the interview after a few more questions. It was over in slightly under an hour. He headed for his glass door, opening, and allowing me access to get out. He thanked me for coming in for the interview and mentioned his office would get back to me in a week or so with their decision. That was it; no decision either way. I had no idea whether he was interested in hiring me or not. Beyond his mention of liking the fact that we had the same birthday, he seemed noncommittal on where he stood on so many of the things we discussed. I thanked him for the interview and his time, rejoined my assistant and headed toward the elevator on the other side of the floor. On the way back to the elevator, I glanced once more around the office floor, noticing all the offices and cubicles appeared full now, most likely brokers returning from a meeting or lunch.

My assistant and I left their office and rode the elevator in silence. I wasn't ready to talk yet, just thinking over the last hour in my head. As we made our way down Market Street toward the van, I felt good about the interview and how it had gone. As we headed out of the city toward home, I felt it was a real mystery what the manager thought. The answer would not be revealed to me until a week or so later.

Keeping the Faith

"Faith in oneself is the best and safest course."

—*Michelangelo*

The following week went by fairly quickly. I continued to work at Vanguard as I finished some night courses I started earlier that summer. When time allowed, I enjoyed the beautiful weather with family and friends. Later that same week, another letter arrived from one of the last two remaining firms I applied to and not heard back from yet. My assistant opened it and held it out for me to read. *"We regret to inform you at this time."* At least this manager signed it, and that was all I needed to see. She put the letter in the file we kept for responses. I had now heard back from six of the seven firms where I applied. Only one of the six was still alive, figuratively speaking, at least to me. It had been so long since the remaining application was mailed, I had no idea if it was even breathing, or if it had already been passed over and tossed in the nearest receptacle, or assigned to the "to be shredded" pile.

Now, the abundant enthusiasm I maintained up to this point was slowly being replaced by a more realistic assessment of my situation. After viewing the letter that just arrived, I began to sense how truly difficult it can be to obtain a position with a brokerage firm. Looking back, I knew that establishing goals was important when I decided I wanted to be a money manager. They were goals I thought might lead to interviews and seemed to be meshing nicely together. I figured three interviews out of the seven firms where I applied were impressive statistics in any field. I began to wonder if I was missing something. Was it my approach, or the fact that I did not let them know I was disabled in my cover letter or application up front?

Mulling over various possibilities in my head, I realized there were probably a few things I may have underestimated; two things I couldn't control. One was an employer's mindset hiring a significantly physically challenged employee, especially one without the use of their hands, arms or legs. Beyond my resume, and the roughly one-hour interview I was afforded with the three interviewing firms, they knew nothing about me. I thought I had presented myself well, and did my best to assure them that my lack of physical ability shouldn't have any bearing. *Was that enough?*

Were they, as employers, seeing beyond the youthful, confident image I portrayed, looking further in the future for this individual? Maybe they were wondering, *"Who is this injured person, one who has to rely on so many things to make it to work? Would he be able to maintain stable health? Have his assistants show up every day? Could he count on all his unique medical equipment functioning properly, just to get to the office? Let alone perform his job and meet our expectations? Is he worth the risk, considering we have other applicants who are just as fired up and eager, but not so limited physically?"*

I realized that regardless of how well I presented myself, how strong and articulate I tried to come off, some employers may be unable to get beyond my wheelchair and the potential liability my paralysis may represent in their mind. All these thoughts, and others, I'm sure swirled in some of the interviewing managers' heads. I understood their concerns. I felt healthy and energetic and tried to present that, but realized others might not feel as confident as me in these areas. I knew it would not be easy to convey how fired up and ready I was, sitting motionless in a large electric chair. I was very fortunate to appear still relatively healthy, though my musculature had diminished quite a bit. I still sat tall, my appearance thankfully not bearing too many remnants of my accident, beyond the obvious. Being able to articulate to some degree may have also helped to present me, as somewhat of a lesser risk, as communicating well is important in this field. It was impossible to know what they were thinking, but I worked hard to address what I felt may be potential concerns as best as I could.

Other injured patients I met in the hospital and kept in touch with were not as fortunate health-wise as me. A few were sick quite regularly. Some had been back in the hospital several times for various spinal-cord injury related issues in the approximately eighteen months since all of us were sent home or to an assisted living facility. Fortunately, I had remained healthy, no hospital stays or sickness, but that was me. Some potential employers might be more understanding and knowledgeable regarding disabilities because of friends or family members with physical or mental limitations. Ironically, they could also be harder to be hired by, having stronger perspectives on what is involved, and the challenges faced by one with an acute disability. While sympathetic, even compassionate, the reality was the position I was seeking required stable, revenue-generating employees, to help contribute to the branch offices bottom line. I could only hope I was convincing enough.

I shared with the firms that granted interviews that I hadn't missed any days beyond what I scheduled off while working at Vanguard. In an interviewer's mind, that would still leave uncertainty about the future in the weeks, months and years ahead. I'm sure that's common in most interviewers' minds when assessing anyone applying for a position, disabilities or not. Merrill Lynch's mindset was what counted now, and whether or not I was even worth the risk. Not only due to my disability but whether I could even become a successful revenue-generating stockbroker, helping clients who had entrusted money to the firm and me.

Another thing I couldn't control was the economy. Information concerning this industry was hard to come by, and coming out of recession, I had no solid idea of where any firm stood on hiring. Armed with these new insights, my earlier enthusiasm 'that things were going great' shifted down somewhat. Brokerage firms, at the time, rarely advertised job openings in the employment sections of local or national papers unless they were a small and unrecognizable business, starting out. The ones I wanted to work for were all large and well established; their branches usually full, with maybe the occasional position available. You would never know that without knowing someone inside. I didn't have those connections or knowledge. So, like many others, I just sent applications, hoping to be there at the right place at the right time.

I had not heard back from Merrill as a week passed. I was still working at Vanguard and had received a small raise in the process. I had not yet considered whether I would go down a path of eventually applying for a full-time position. Another week flew by and still no word.

Two days later, after arriving home from work, a letter was on my computer desk in my bedroom. The embossed return address showed it was from Merrill Lynch. I hadn't noticed it before letting my assistant leave for the day. My parents, who thoughtfully placed it there, were entertaining guests who had come for dinner that night. I couldn't stand the anticipation, and went into the kitchen and asked my mother to open it when she had a moment. She excused herself from her company and came in.

My heart raced. This letter and its contents would determine a lot concerning my future. As she held the letter out, I scanned its contents. Merrill Lynch was offering me a position at their flagship office in Center City! I was elated; all my hopes and dreams seemed to be coming to fruition. The letter went into further detail concerning my starting salary for eighteen months. The salary was impressive, and competitive with the top starting salaries of new hires in the industry.

The offering also included good health benefits. As I read further, my initial enthusiasm began to wane a little.

Further down near the bottom of the correspondence, it made reference to a mandatory three-week training program I would have to attend at their corporate training center in Princeton, New Jersey. That revelation set me back a bit in my tracks. They expected me to go away and stay for three weeks at their privately owned facility that was about two hours away. Also, I would be attending classes from eight in the morning every day until five at night. These classes would be followed by company sponsored events and dinners afterward. How was I going to coordinate all that?

After the injury, when home from the hospitals and rehabs, I had never been away for more than two nights in a row. Only for weekend trips to the shore, often returning tired and sunburned, with an equally tired assistant or girlfriend who made the trip with me on her own. Now, they were expecting me to go away for twenty-four hours a day for three weeks straight, a difficult thing to arrange logistically on such short notice. My work assistant's longest shifts were mostly eight hours in duration, nowhere near what going away would require.

Now, after landing my dream job, one I had spent so many months trying to prepare for, a major hurdle emerged out of the blue. Initially, reading the compensation package, I thought the final lap was completed, and the finish line in view. This mandatory condition was quite a surprise. I was thankful they hired me, but would I now have to decline their offer? Would this requirement be too difficult to overcome? At this stage, my mind was on fire, running through my assistant ranks to try and determine who may have the flexibility to accompany me. Even worse, I knew I would need a minimum of two assistants, to split the time between them. To expect one assistant to work alone was ludicrous; themselves, they wouldn't be able to handle the strain. Not to mention, they would be utterly exhausted. It was a lot to pull together, but I would have to somehow. Too much was hanging in the balance.

The following day, I learned the next training program was two weeks away, starting in early August. Fortunately, several of my assistants were college students. One was already working with me at Vanguard, and the other was assisting in the mornings, as well as some nights and weekends. I was hoping against hope that possibly they would be able to go, as their classes wouldn't resume until a week after the training session ended. After getting more details from Merrill, I learned they didn't have any classes on weekends. I realized that meant all three of us could leave Friday after classes and not have to return until Monday morning. Hopefully, it might take some pressure off, and if compensated well, they might be interested in this arrangement. Getting those weekends off would help.

After discussing the situation with them, and offering a generous bonus for doing this, I was able to arrange it. The assistants who would accompany me found the proposal more palatable, upon learning they would have weekends off. They were excited for me; they knew how hard I had worked to realize this opportunity. I was thrilled that everything was coming together.

I knew I needed to inform Vanguard that I was leaving. This wouldn't be easy. Not only had they treated me well, I was also fortunate to make some good friends there. When I did notify, a day after receiving the offer letter from Merrill, they weren't upset and were happy for me. They assured me, by leaving, that it would not disrupt anything within the department. They had others coming and going in the same capacity. I said goodbye to my friends and manager after fulfilling my two-week promise and left for Princeton and Merrill's training facility the following Sunday.

My assistants and I packed what gear we thought necessary (yes, including extra clothes, deodorant, and cologne) and made it to the training facility in two hours. While being lowered on my van lift in their parking area, I glanced around, amazed at how beautiful and impressive the main building appeared. Learning the details before arrival, I knew it was a three-story building with over 337 private lodging rooms. A picturesque five-acre lake graced this 275-acre facility, complete with fountains and manicured courtyards.

All three of us checked into the two adjoining rooms that Merrill hospitably provided. After putting our bags down, the three of us headed for the elevators in the direction of their auditorium. Everyone invited to this three-week training session was supposed to meet there, and we arrived at the facility with fifteen minutes to spare. Approaching the auditorium, I wheeled toward one of the many doors leading in. Smiling ushers greeted my assistants, and me as they escorted us to an accessible section. After seating us, an usher handed each of my assistants an itinerary.

All three of us sat in silence, for the most part, looking around inside this large, lavish room, a little taken back by the enormity of the moment. The massive onstage screen was emblazoned with Merrill's world-renowned symbol, a huge bull, as light music filtered in the background. When the auditorium appeared mostly full, pumped up trainers took the stage to begin the introduction. Armed with a colorful presentation, they ran through the training center's amenities. They started off showing pictures of their workout rooms, multiple cafeterias, various dining rooms, and many activities, including beautiful outdoor walking trails. They finished their amenities presentation with spectacular shots of their well-lit lake and fountains at night.

This part of the presentation made this place seem more like a resort, just a great place to eat, relax and stay for a couple of weeks in pampered luxury. However, it became very apparent early on that it was also a training program, and this facility was out to make a big statement. That statement being: Merrill stands alone.

Once the amenities portion of the presentation concluded, they rolled out the three-week training program. Only a few screenshots in, as they went over the curriculum, it became very apparent that my time here would not be a vacation. More and more, it was looking like a very in-depth program that would require a lot of attention and effort. The presentation was covering everything about Merrill. From its products, sales techniques, compliance measures and internal safe-guards, on to investment strategies, how to build a book of business, operate the software running their proprietary client and investment programs, to a host of other topics. As I sat there listening with my two assistants, I realized that this was the big time, the most touted training program on Wall Street, and they were expecting a lot from new hires like me.

The magnitude of what lay ahead was starting to sink in. Until I received that offer letter, I didn't have any idea about Merrill's training program, or what was required of new money manager hires. Going in, I had no concrete ideas about what the training would cover. For that matter, before my assistants said they could go that I'd even be sitting here on a Sunday afternoon (the only weekend day required), two hours from home for the next three weeks. Nothing much beyond the pre-conceived ideas I had arrived with, thinking perhaps the training consisted of some courses covering how to build a book of business, some mock client calls for practice and learn about their proprietary products. Then back to their flagship office in Philadelphia and start trading on my never used Series 7 license.

As I continued listening and watching the presentation, the goals I had established, while not easy, looked remedial compared to the new responsibilities I had just shouldered. With Merrill Lynch, my compensation after my first eighteen months would be purely commission based, with no paid holidays, vacation or sick days. Anyone in this field knows what I'm referring to and how your compensation is structured. As an employee, you are judged by your performance, and you start over at the end of every month. Besides being ethical and honest, not violating Merrill's principles, rules or SEC regulations, there are some basic tenets to not being fired. Beyond strong back-office and technical support, sales assistance, and in-house market analysts covering investments and economies to draw upon for support, most everything else falls on you. Who you call, interact with for business, products offered to clients, revenues, commissions generated, how you go about building your book of business all adds up to two things. How much in assets do you have in Merrill's house and what are you ethically generating in the way of revenues on not only those assets, but on the new assets and clients you better be adding to those numbers. I was thrilled. Though all of the course curricula presented a new learning curve for me, and much steeper than what I was exposed to previously, I knew I would learn a lot. It sounded a little overwhelming, but I was young, healthy and curious. I wanted to find out more about myself and what was possible for me in this field. This position would be a strong test and lucrative as well.

Now, for the first time in my life, I was pushing the envelope career-wise. I would draw upon things I had learned in my game of life so far, add to those, and work hard to be successful in a tough industry. Mike had given me a chance. I didn't want to let him or Merrill down.

Sure, being a good guy or a funny person are excellent traits to bring into any company, where co-workers and managers might appreciate your personality and quips. In some companies, if your performance is sub-par or buried in organizational layers, perhaps you get lucky enough, and there are others around you helping to carry your workload. If you're fortunate, you may skate through, able to blend into the shadows, unscathed by performance shortcomings because you were friends with the boss, or people liked you enough. This is not the reality on Wall Street.

Nice guy or not, whether you retain your job and your money management career is solely up to you and what you generate for the firm is the primary determinant. In the process, you try to do well by your clients and build a book of business by referrals and cold calls, working to attract new business. I later learned it cost Merrill Lynch, at the time, about $40,000 to run one new trainee through this intensive program. Today, I'm sure it would probably be twice that cost, especially if they still had the same training facility open, which they no longer do. The manager who hired me, Michael Boland, had reached out to give me a hand and an opportunity to build a career on Wall Street. Though on the surface, the risks he was taking with a relatively inexperienced and untested guy in this business, paralyzed from the shoulders down, I'm sure appeared significant. Thankfully, Mike saw more.

I knew I was setting myself up with bigger challenges in my life, but after overcoming so much I didn't feel intimidated to continue on the path I had visualized for myself over a year ago. It wouldn't be easy; the position required an assistant driving me in an over-sized van, over an hour away at all times of the year, in the densest part of Philadelphia, working on the thirty-fifth floor of a high rise. I would be trying to build a book of business without any real contacts and would be relying on many assistants to help me in the process. But the reality of what lay ahead didn't matter. I would now be working at Merrill, and they were carrying me for eighteen months, on a good salary, and were willing to give me a chance. I felt very fortunate to have landed a position with the top firm I wanted. Many things needed to come together to get this far. Again, it was up to me, to see where this would lead.

After three weeks, consisting of a lot of classroom work, training was over. I had met some amazing people from all over the country and different parts of the world, making several good friends in the process. During the entire training program, my assistants were treated wonderfully, everyone appreciating their effort and hard work. Merrill Lynch exceeded our expectations, providing an unforgettable experience for all. Like myself, new Merrill trainees would return to the respective offices that hired them, hoping to apply some of our newfound knowledge and build a client base in the process. Merrill threw a big going-away party at the end, complete with musicians, top class food, and drink.

This picture is of my graduating training class at Merrill Lynch. I am in the middle and the gentleman on my left was a former CEO of Adidas.

Personally, I was glad to return home and get to work. It had been a non-stop, information-packed whirlwind—coupled with entertaining events to break up the educational rigor. It was late Friday and my first day in the office was to be the following Monday. It left me a few days to wind down and mentally rehash all the things they had thrown at me in those three weeks.

My first weeks at Merrill went by smoothly. I began to familiarize myself with the forty or so brokers who occupied the entire top floor of the building, and Merrill's proprietary trading systems, as well as their firm offerings. My assistant and I organized our desk area, from the computer placement to the new files. Mike thoughtfully arranged for a phone line to be set up, for my assistant and me to share, using separate headsets. The client books and other material we would need were placed on her side of the cubicle, providing an easier way to get the material necessary for a particular call or client. We began making a list of potential clients we would call, starting out with family and friends and hone our phone skills in the process.

I tried to stay on top of the markets since deciding on this career. This centered the majority of my conversations on what was impacting the markets at the time, and on investments they were already holding elsewhere. I was having fun, and in the process, learning many new things. Some of my most valuable insights came from seasoned brokers in our office. Several of them had been with Merrill nearly their entire career, some spanning thirty years and they were invaluable sources. Their brokerage experiences ran the gamut; from the markets they had faced, to the changes and evolution of the industry over the years. I would probe them on individual companies and market cycles, while their eyes shone with excitement recounting some incredible stock picks they had made, and some markets they had called. In some cases, making small fortunes for their clients, or saving them from devastating losses. They spoke of the advancements in technology they experienced at Merrill and in the industry at large. They also shared how politics, regulations, tax laws, interest rates, wars, oil embargos, and other factors impacted markets.

In this environment, I experienced a priceless education, not only from listening to their stories but by watching the markets and the news impacting them daily. Working with clients was invaluable, and the knowledge I gained in this industry could never have been duplicated in a classroom setting or out of a book.

As time went by, I began to develop a client base and learn from my mistakes and failures, as well as my successes and victories. I became more attuned to what worked out in an investment I had made initially, and what may have changed the scenario. The markets often have their ideas on how to interpret various events, as everyone has experienced. Whether interest rate tightening or loosening, weak or strong economic data, markets often have a mind of their own and the reactions can be quite extreme on occasion. The only drug that has worked consistently to bring euphoria or calm in the last ten years to the markets was that administered by the FED in the way of excessive money printing and abnormally low interest rates over an extended period. Now that supposed cure is beginning to look highly suspect.

Accident fails to halt young broker

About a week before last Oct. 19, D. Bradley Smith and his wife got what proved to be a good piece of advice from their stockbroker.

"He said that he didn't know how much longer the bull market would last and it might be a good idea to pull out and hang tight for a little while and see what happens," Smith recalled.

"So that's what we did."

No sooner had the Smiths sold their modest holdings in eight telecommunications companies than the stock market crashed. The Smiths had gotten out just in time. And a few days later, they bought back the same stocks at prices far below what they had just sold them for.

"We made out pretty well on that deal," said Smith, 29, a programmer analyst for Hunt Manufacturing Co.

Maybe it was beginner's luck; Rippy only started work as a registered broker on Sept. 16. But his boss, Michael J. Boland, Merrill Lynch's resident vice president here, sees a bright future for him.

"He's a first-quintile producer," said Boland, meaning that Rippy ranks in the top 20 percent of Merrill Lynch's freshman brokers in Philadelphia.

"Because of his personal situation, he's obviously very focused."

"I didn't hire him because I felt sorry for him," emphasized Boland. "That didn't enter into it. He's just unbelievable."

Last July, Rippy accepted Boland's job offer and, after training in Philadelphia and Princeton, began work in mid-September.

By PETER BINZEN

On business

His day begins at 5 a.m., when a nursing assistant, a college student living in the Rippys' home, wakes him up, shaves him, gets him to perform certain exercises designed for quadriplegics, then dresses him and gets his breakfast. At 7 o'clock, Jennifer Tyrrell arrives, wheels him into his specially fitted blue van (the CAT Fund paid for the conversion work) and drives him to the office, usually arriving before 8:30.

She parks on the north side of Market Street just east of 16th Street, in a slot that police have reserved for Rippy.

With his nursing assistant opening the mail, fielding phone calls and getting his lunch, the broker works a full day, returning home about 6 p.m. There, another assistant takes over until 10 p.m. or thereabouts, when it's lights out.

"It's a constant run," Rippy said of the time required to perform the smallest tasks. "When I get home at 6, we run until 9 o'clock. The biggest thing you have to learn is patience. You're always relying on other people."

He loves the stock market too much to fear the future. "It's terrific," he said. "Always something different. And you can't learn enough."

For a stockbroker, his kind of disability is no real handicap, Rippy insists. "It's not a physical game," he said of the brokerage business, "it's a mental game. And I have the endurance. I can keep the long hours."

Boland agreed. He said Rippy attends all staff functions and has missed only one day of work.

Excerpt from an article that appeared in the business section of the major Philadelphia daily paper.

One year, the market would behave one way on similar data, but several years later or less, the market would interpret the information with a different spin, and produce the opposite result. The constantly evolving nature and complexities of the financial markets kept me interested. They also bring their lessons in humility, regardless of what was expected going into an investment, there were times the results didn't always pan out as I planned. Everyone in the investment business can readily attest to this.

What I noticed among most brokers, seasoned or otherwise, was that the investment choices they recommended were often based on their personal interests, and most would become quite astute in a couple of industries. They would follow them closely and invest in those sectors if it appeared advantageous to their clients. If various sectors were out of favor on Wall Street, as is to be expected at times, you would look for other opportunities to approach clients with and expand into these areas, depending on the market cycle. There were times to consider consumer stocks, International, Emerging Market, defensive stocks, healthcare companies, commodity-based or "landscape changing" stocks, like the red-hot tech sector before the 2000 crash. Today's "transforming and disrupting" technology-based companies have drawn a lot of interest. There were always many things to be aware of, as you may imagine, that could impact investments well beyond the scope of this book.

Still Riding the Bull

*"There is only one side of the market and it is not the
bull side or the bear side, but the right side."*

— *Jesse Livermore*

I WAS NOW ON COMMISSION, my year and a half of salary had just ended,
and my book of business was more than compensating me for the difference. My income was now covered by my growing clientele list, and
new ideas I approached them with. My system seemed to be working.
My assistants were becoming more proficient in multiple areas; from
filling out order tickets, to taking good client meeting notes and an-
ticipating what information I needed at different times during a phone
call. On many occasions prior to a business call, I would have the assistant retrieve information perceived as relevant to that particular client,
trying to anticipate their concerns or needs.

Over time, the interactions with my assistants became almost seamless. Very few of my clients ever came to know of my disability. It was not to be deceitful, simply that it was irrelevant in most cases to share, as I had been hired as their money manager. Ironically, it was important for me to know about their health issues or concerns, as different investment considerations had to be factored in, whether involving estates, trusts, and income streams, among other things.

Going into my third year with Merrill, they had hired only two other brokers at this office since I had started. The third person they hired was coming off another career; Reggie Wilkes, a former linebacker with the Philadelphia Eagles and Atlanta Falcons. He was the first former professional athlete they had hired in our office since I started. Reggie was an easy-going, modest and funny guy. After playing ten years in the NFL, he had many stories to share. Some involved former players he faced on the gridiron as a linebacker, on to his life as an NFL player. His stories were always amusing and light.

With the office on the thirty-fifth floor, there was always a concern in the back of my mind as to what I would do if the power went out, disabling the elevators or worse, a fire. One day, fire ravaged a taller building on the other side of Market Street, up one block from us. Fortunately, it was put out quickly and had only been on a few floors after working hours. Thankfully, no one was hurt, though it did sink into all those working in the high rises downtown, that it was a potential concern.

I said to Reggie the following day, "Hey Reggie..." and he knew immediately what I was going to bring up. "Don't worry Rip; I have your back. I'll get you out." He was aware what I was referring to; if a building fire occurred and it was serious, there was a real possibility of needing him to throw me over his back and go down the thirty-five floors of steps on foot. I knew it wouldn't be a fun journey, hustled like a sack of potatoes over somebody's shoulder. However, at 6'5", 235 pounds and still in good shape, I knew that he was my best shot. At least I may get out alive and still intact. My electric chair would have to stay. At 250 pounds alone, there was no way to get it down in an emergency. That was okay. There wasn't a choice if there was a fire, and it was a small sacrifice where one's life was involved. In my world, though, a pretty big deal, the difference between some semblance of independence and having the ability to maneuver unaided, as opposed to having to rely on an assistant to wheel me around. As mentioned earlier, it took many months to get a chair, due to insurance and all the requirements involved. I could be without a power chair that fit my needs for quite some time. Hopefully, I wouldn't be faced with that dilemma. For those reading this book who have been adversely affected by losing necessary equipment, providing some level of independence, my heart goes out to you. I understand what's involved.

My days at Merrill rolled on the weeks turning into months, and the months into my fourth year. Teamwork between my assistants and me was essential so we could best meet our clients' needs in the process. That it not to say issues didn't invariably crop up, and plenty did, whether it was due to an assistant who couldn't make it in, to a chair or van malfunction. I simply realized that the easiest way to move forward was to put negative and self-defeating thoughts out of my mind as quickly as possible. Doing so helped me think through the problem with more clarity and focus.

My office routine varied little, consisting mostly of working with clients, discussing various investments, and trying to bring in new business from prospects or client referrals. The office was usually vibrant much like it had been for my initial interview when I went there wide-eyed and a bit intimidated. Starting my fourth year, I felt more seasoned and knowledgeable in a variety of different ways. I had also obtained my insurance license two years earlier and was now able to discuss with clients various insurance products, from life to health coverage. I was helping them manage their retirement assets, trust assets, taxable assets, annuities, some insurance and having fun doing it. I had learned other things as well, from covered call writing, hedging with options, barbell and bullet bond positioning, among many other strategies.

I was making more money, continually learning and keeping up, in so many different areas, helping me to grow in this field. I now felt vindicated and was happy with how things were working out. I enjoyed some good friendships at Merrill, all hardworking and fun guys to be around. When dealing with their clients, they were all great talkers and storytellers. Everyone I knew who worked there was very conscientious of what they recommended to clients, and kept their best interests in mind, from what I gathered.

By cultivating and maintaining client trust, it led to long-term relationships that would provide me the flexibility to explore other possibilities down the line if I wanted. Though not every strategy, every stock recommendation went as expected, the client relationship, friendship, and trust that was earned over the years were the most important factors. Of course, they all wanted to make money, every stock to be the next Amazon, Apple, Alphabet, Facebook, Microsoft or Tesla, but they knew that wasn't realistic. Many had already made and saved money through their working years and if retired, the preservation of that wealth was paramount over hot stock ideas.

Some other good friendships I made at Merrill were based on a common enjoyment of boxing. Boxing was a sport I enjoyed watching, an individualistic sport, just you against your opponent. It required incredible stamina, skill, a lot of heart, and a ferocious desire to win to be among the greats. I wasn't enamored by the dangers in the sport, sadly seeing some of the former greats in various stages of cognitive decline. Not a good comparison by any means, I was a wrestler from seventh grade through varsity in high school, on to intramurals in college. I could, to a small degree, appreciate what these athletes put their bodies through in preparation for a fight, or match in my case. I distinctly remember my lungs burning like they were on fire from running and training, with every muscle in my body fatigued from the strenuous workouts. Though the wrestling analogy isn't even close to what boxers endure—almost like comparing apples to oranges—I felt that feeling again after being hired by Merrill Lynch. The joy and exhilaration of getting that shot and the struggles I went through to get that chance.

One of the brokers I came to know well in the office was a guy named Ted. The two of us enjoyed talking about fights and viewing matches when possible. Ted and I, among my brothers and friends on occasion, witnessed some of the greatest fights of the day in Atlantic City. I was fortunate to meet many involved in the sport, from the biggest promoters, to several world heavyweight champions, on down through the weight classes.

Enjoyed meeting the future president Donald Trump at one of his
pre-fight events when he was co-promoting a Mike Tyson fight.
He was very cordial and personable. I enjoyed discussing my career
at Merrill Lynch and Tyson's fight that night with him.

Sharing some words with boxing promoter Don
King at ringside before a Tyson fight.
Pictured from L-R: Don King, Butterbean (boxer) in back,
Ted (Merrill Lynch friend) and an assistant.

Pictured with English boxing champion Frank Bruno,
moments before attending a Tyson fight.

With Larry Holmes, former Heavyweight Champion, outside the
Mark G. Etess Arena in Atlantic City. Pictured L-R: My brother
Ross, me, my brother Paul (behind chair), and Larry Holmes.

Spending some time with Tommy "the Duke" Morrison, a former
heavyweight champion. What a powerful puncher; out of 343 fights in
his amateur and professional career, Tommy had 315 knockouts.

Had a very enjoyable and lengthy conversation with Bobby Czyz, a former
light heavyweight champion, a very cerebral and interesting guy. We discussed
one of his fights that I attended the previous month among other things.

Sitting ringside right before a Tyson Heavyweight Championship fight. Mike was wearing his trademark top, basically a white bath towel with a hole cut out for his head. Don King is seen clapping in the background.

Meeting the legendary Sugar Ray Leonard. What a great, warm guy to converse with. Enjoyed discussing his career and pursuits. Glasses and goatee artwork courtesy of my talented niece in her youth.

Ringside watching Iron Mike Tyson destroy an opponent who is getting
a standing eight count from the referee after a vicious attack.

Equally interesting to me was meeting many well-known and successful figures. Whether they were involved in film, pageants, televi-
sion, art, promotions, business, investing or activism, I made a point
to meet them. We would share some words; whether discussing fights,
past or later that night, on to what they were currently doing in their
pursuits. I was impressed with the time that was afforded to me, and
their interest in our conversation, often asking multiple questions and
listening closely to my answers.

In Atlantic City, enjoying some time with Liam Neeson prior
to a Mike Tyson fight. Liam also boxed in Ireland, winning the
Northern Ireland Juvenile Championship three times.

Exchanging a few words with Carl Icahn at a pre-
fight event hosted by Donald Trump.

Some conversations, Ted and I initiated, grabbing the attention of those we wanted to meet and others would walk up, joining in the exchanges or just listen. It was fun meeting people who were prominent in their respective fields.

Pictured with Gene Hackman before a Tyson fight. It was amazing reminiscing with such a legend regarding some of his movies I have enjoyed.

Conversing with Jesse Jackson at a Trump-sponsored pre-fight party.

Pictured with LeRoy Neiman, an American artist known for his brilliantly colored, expressionist paintings and screen prints of athletes, musicians, and sporting events. LeRoy was present to do a painting of Mike Tyson.

Talking with Suzette Charles, a former Miss America. Suzette was not only beautiful, but engaging, as we discussed what she was doing after her reign as Miss America.

Wonderful time sitting ringside with a former Saturday Night Live
star, Joe Piscopo, for the Holyfield vs. Foreman fight. Joe and I hit
it off well and I was impressed with what a great guy he is.

I would briefly share with those we met at these events that my disability was due to a car accident, to satisfy that curiosity, and move the
conversation on to my position at Merrill. After a few minutes, I would
ask what they were currently pursuing. Some conversations were long
and others shorter depending on who was nearby vying for their time,
calling them away for various reasons. After taking the time for a picture together, some nice parting words, we moved on to make other
acquaintances.

Exploring Other
Career Options

⌒

WHILE I WAS ENJOYING MY time at Merrill Lynch, now into my fourth year, from a logistical standpoint, the long daily commutes were starting to take a toll. In addition, the safety concerns of working on the thirty-fifth floor began to take on more significance. Though this was the financial district, and many of the biggest firms in the city were represented in a roughly six-block area on Market Street near City Hall, it still wasn't the safest place in the world. Philadelphia, like many major cities, had been impacted by necessary budget cutbacks, most often during recessionary periods. This equated to fewer Philadelphia officers on duty, particularly several officers who had been assigned to my block over the previous three years. They were always a welcome sight, fun to talk to, helpful and friendly, their presence alone helped assure that crime in this area remained at a minimum. Now, the police presence was no longer visible. Though the officers never had to protect me from any trouble, having a couple of towering law enforcement officers, both about six foot, five inches tall, working near my building, was a reassuring sight. Now, parking was more difficult without their assistance directing my van into its space on a busy Market Street when arriving, and the safety factor had dropped.

Over the next several months, it was easy to notice the changes; there was more loitering and panhandling, coupled with more nefarious behavior. It wasn't unusual for someone to stagger up to my van after work, a brown bag in one hand smelling like liquor, when my assistant and I exited the building at night. While we were more than happy to help people with difficult lives, providing funds to further addictions was not something we planned on doing. I felt a little more vulnerable, especially at night. I didn't feel comfortable exposing my assistants or myself to this potentially more dangerous environment. Also, there were now fewer officers to help guide traffic when city stop lights were not working, finding us mired in traffic jams getting to or from work.

I received a call from a friend, who was a former Merrill broker who had been employed with the same Philadelphia office as me. He had left Merrill two years earlier, to manage a branch office of a competing firm, and called to discuss an opportunity with me that I wanted to consider carefully. The position was located on the outskirts of Philadelphia in a safer area and closer to my home. By leaving Merrill, I would reduce my commuting time by over an hour daily and my office would be on the third floor of the building, a safety consideration in case I had to evacuate due to a fire or a power outage.

Equally important, like Merrill, this firm also had a rock solid and well-respected reputation. It was founded in Philadelphia in 1865, and over the subsequent years, had relocated out of the city. My friend spoke of the opportunities this firm offered. Having worked at Merrill, he was very familiar with both companies and as a result was able to provide strong comparative data. He had been a successful broker at Merrill and had decided to leave for better opportunities, opportunities he was now interested in sharing with me.

While at Merrill, he sat near my desk, and we would discuss the markets, our weekend plans, sports, and about any topic one would engage in with a co-worker you liked but only knew casually. He knew that Merrill was my start in the brokerage business, where he had begun as well. Ironically, his firm was one I had not applied to in the beginning of my job search. Four years earlier, they probably wouldn't have been as interested as they were now, being an unknown element starting out.

To even consider the switch to this firm, the overall employment package, and benefits had to be appealing to not only me but also to my clients. Naturally, I was hoping many clients would follow me to this new firm. The fact that my clients would enjoy lower commissions for two years, while I would receive a more lucrative compensation percentage on trades, made for a strong incentive for my departing Merrill.

Considering everything, there were many more pluses than minuses. It was not only a safer environment on a much lower office floor and closer to home, but the private office they offered was also much more spacious, something my assistants liked as well.

I began working on a letter to my clients, letting them know of my transition to the new firm, and the advantages they would have if they decided to join me. I knew I would need to meet with my manager, to discuss my departure.

I knew it wouldn't be an easy trip to Mike's office. I felt bad leaving, but upon discussing the new location, lower floor, and safer environment, he felt it was a wise decision. He was aware of the dangers of being in a wheelchair in a high rise, especially in an office thirty-five floors off the ground. He also understood my long daily commutes and appreciated what my assistants had to accomplish just to get me to my desk every morning.

Eight years earlier, Mike had hired the manager who had recruited me and had retained a positive opinion of him when he left. Mike, like most managers or brokers, had also switched firms in his past, which is not uncommon for those pursuing greater opportunities. Though I was considered a successful broker by different measures, my departure would have a negligible impact on the office's revenues, due to the other producing agents in our branch.

It was tough saying goodbye to my co-workers. They understood why I was leaving. Mike recognized the advantages for me, as I thanked him for the opportunity. I could tell he knew I meant it. His eyes reflected wisdom and compassion, a rare combination in this highly competitive industry, where compassion and ethics are sometimes interchanged with ego and greed. As mentioned earlier, I had watched the movie *Wall Street*, and later, *The Wolf of Wall Street*. After working at Merrill, and knowing many of the brokers in this office, I found these Hollywood portrayals to be the opposite of my experience. Unfortunately, there will always be those who tarnish the industry's image. In my office, many nice guys from Reggie, Ted, Vernon, Jim, Bob, Mike, and others filled our ranks, making my departure, from a co-worker perspective, bittersweet.

Only years later while writing this book, did it dawn on me that perhaps when I wheeled into Mike's penthouse office for my interview, he saw more than just a young, disabled guy with big dreams who was looking for a shot. Not aware of his service record then, Mike had served in Vietnam. Just speculating now, perhaps, I reminded him of a few of the guys that he had met or served with. Some coming home disabled, still young, confident and ambitious, setting goals and working hard to achieve them. Mike knew that many coming home never got that chance, that one shot for a career they wanted. Possibly, he saw that dream and focus in my eyes, not unlike many who had just returned home from service, or were just released from hospitals and rehabilitation centers.

Though I had never served, he probably could relate to my situation, a guy just wanting to move on after overcoming so much, start a career and get back to families and friends. Mike, God bless him, saw beyond my chair, beyond my setback, and was willing to take a chance. Sadly, he passed away of cancer several years back. Our paths didn't cross again after I left Merrill, and not for any particular reason. I became aware of his funeral after it took place from the obituary notice someone had sent to me, asking if this was my former manager. I was disappointed I hadn't known sooner. I would have wanted to go to his funeral and pay my respects.

I think it is important to acknowledge Mike and hope others in a hiring capacity will consider giving a person with a disability who is looking for an opportunity, a chance. Though I had worked hard and set goals that I eventually accomplished which led to my interviews, I still feel blessed that Mike opened the door to my career. His gesture subsequently led to the incredible opportunities I realized not only at Merrill, but other firms afterward. Also, I would like to acknowledge the wonderful clients, co-workers, and friends I have met along the way.

Life after Merrill

I STARTED WITH THE NEW firm the following week. I jumped into the position, enjoying the location, private office, and compensation package. Cutting an hour off my daily commute was beautiful, and being closer to home made more sense if something happened. Commuting to Philadelphia during all seasons, for four years, was no easy task and tough enough. Whether due to snow and ice in the winter, rain in the spring or fall, the heat, and humidity of the summer, with an assistant driving, my commute to the city on densely packed highways and roads was demanding.

Experiencing another big Northeast United States snowstorm.
The picture was taken after my van and long driveway
were shoveled out so I could depart to work.

With the new firm, I felt revitalized. It was hard not to, considering the advantages that switching represented. I had a strong book of business and was grateful that the majority of my clients followed me. My assistants also enjoyed the shorter commute and the new office located outside of the city, in an upscale corporate business park. The private office also lent itself to getting around in my chair more easily due to its spacious layout, making it simpler to access client material. My clients were happier with their lower fees per trade, and I was pleased with what the higher commission structure meant to my paycheck. This firm's office was smaller in square footage than Merrill, had fewer seasoned brokers, but nonetheless, it was still a fun and ambitious group.

As we settled in, the next few years went by quickly. Assistants had to move on occasionally, now newly minted college graduates, armed with a diploma and some work experience. They were ready to jump into the job market and pursue their own careers. Assistants leaving my employ would help train new hires, whether for morning shifts, office work or evening shifts. Those hired would typically end up working with me for several years. They enjoyed the office environment and position, realizing how important work experience is in a challenging job market.

My assistants and I continued to evolve in the brokerage industry together, while technological expansion in the financial sector grew at a rapid pace as well. Many firms were sinking hundreds of millions of dollars into their trading systems for brokers and fund managers, continually upgrading when budgets allowed. As a result, it was also becoming common for clients to explore and trade in the markets independently, using a financial firms website and online trading tools. Every new assistant I hired had to be better trained and savvier technologically than those they were replacing. The complexity and demands of using continually upgraded software, often utilizing five or six different programs for one client call, was demanding. Switching between programs with only the most subtle of cues from me required an assistant who was sharp, quick on a computer, and could learn rapidly.

Thankfully, they were amazing on average, making my client interactions smoother, sharp and seamless.

Fortunately, as technology advanced, ushering in laptops, tablets, and smartphones meant all of my new hires were good with computers coming in. Having grown up with them at a very young age made their training on complex software programs much easier, and most office assistants would hit the ground running after fairly short training sessions. I would write complimentary referral letters for the ones leaving, and talk to their prospective employers if they wanted.

Over time, it was becoming apparent that many other firms in our industry were starting to offer bigger discount fees on trades. Some commissions on trades were even in the single digits. Firms like E-trade, Schwab, Ameritrade and others were starting to offer investors incredibly steep discounts—discounts impossible for the full-service brokerages to match with their higher overhead costs and commission structures for brokers. While the discount brokers didn't offer advice, there were now more advice-oriented newsletters available than in previous years. The internet was becoming a game changer for the industry, particularly at the full-service firm level. With faster transmission times and expanded internet capabilities, it was easy for anyone to access real-time data on stocks and individual companies. An investor was now able to trade their account online while sitting at home, using different market sources and tools that were previously unavailable to the general public. Many discount brokerage firms also started offering their clientele free software programs to generate their own trading methods and ideas. Now, analysts, brokers and financial companies were competing directly with the myriad of changes the better technologies represented to an independent and astute investor.

Though my clients relied on my advice, there were many avenues to buy additional shares through a discount broker, if they so chose. Some of my clients liked to trade and enjoyed buying or selling securities online, sometimes outside of our firm. Of course, I would've liked if every transaction was placed through me, but they also had their ideas, and

I respected that. I was with a full-service brokerage firm, and though my book of business was growing the headwinds of discount brokers, coupled with stronger internet capabilities, was impacting my revenue stream. Large mutual fund houses like Fidelity and Vanguard were also increasingly competitive, able to take advantage of their tremendous size by offering clients a multitude of product lines—offers that kept growing in scope and were extremely cost-attractive.

In the time since I had left Vanguard, they had expanded their financial services offerings as well. Their large cash inflows and greater concentration on containing costs also meant they could compete with economies of scale unavailable to full-service firms, with their high overhead.

The founder of Vanguard, the legendary John Bogle, had written a thesis while at Princeton on the advantages of low-cost purchase fees on mutual funds, and how significant this was to an investor's portfolio performance. A very straightforward concept and John founded Vanguard on this principal, among other "client friendly" directives. He began offering customers what are known as "no load" mutual funds. This meant no commissions on these products and just the smallest of expense ratios, easily rivaling and in ninety-nine percent of cases, surpassing anyone offering funds in the industry. At their corporate headquarters in Valley Forge, Pennsylvania, Vanguard's name and sterling reputation were well known throughout the tri-state area, a region where a good fifty percent of my clients resided.

Vanguard...Coming Full Circle

⌒

We are what we repeatedly do. Excellence,
then, is not an act, but a habit.

−ARISTOTLE

ONE NIGHT I DECIDED TO hit a local eatery with a girl I had been dat-
ing for some time. About thirty minutes into our meal, I felt a hand
on my shoulder and heard a familiar voice. It happened to be my first
manager at the part-time job I had held at Vanguard years earlier. He
introduced us to his wife, as they pulled up chairs. My girlfriend and I
were eating alone, providing the perfect opportunity to catch up with
my former manager. She hit it off immediately with his wife, both of
them enjoying their talk. His name was also Dave, and he briefed me
on his life and career since I had left Vanguard. He was still employed
there and had moved up the career ladder, now with a whole different
division of the company.

I shared my career with Dave over the subsequent years, and what
had taken place. I kept it light and professional as he listened with interest about Merrill, as well as the other firm. He knew one of the reasons
I had left Vanguard was due to a lack of opportunities to provide clients

with my investment advice and ideas. Dealing independently with my clients was something he remembered was important to me for personal growth. After asking him if anything had changed at Vanguard in that regard since I had left, he mentioned the name of an entirely new department Vanguard had started approximately two years earlier, one that worked with clients directly. This department could provide ideas to clients within reasonable, well thought out, tested parameters and offered strong financial planning as well. The position was salary-driven, with partnership and bonus potential. Not commission-oriented, which caught my interest, and for the clients who decided to transition, they would gain even better discounts than I could offer on purchases and sales. Our conversation shifted to other areas, at which point we both learned we didn't live that far apart. What was amazing was that I had not seen or spoken to Dave since I had left Vanguard, until that night.

Since I had started with Merrill, Vanguard had expanded their campus to accommodate their growth. Their assets under management had grown to almost a trillion by 2006, moving up to around $3.6 trillion as this book goes to print. John Bogle, the founder of Vanguard, retired in 1996, retaining a strong presence there, and keeping an office on campus. His successor, John Brennan, who had reported directly to John Bogle for years, reassuringly maintained the same vision that Bogle had started at Vanguard. When Brennan retired, he was replaced by Bill McNabb, who carried forward the same traditions; maintaining high principles, integrity, and values. Other new changes since I was there ranged from the availability of online trading for clients, along with a host of industry-leading technological and innovative changes. Due to the tremendous size of Vanguard's assets under management and the millions of customer accounts they are handling, Vanguard is the industry leader in mutual funds. Merrill, when I left, was the industry leader in client brokerage accounts and still is today.

Vanguard is one of the lowest cost providers in the industry, and one of the first to pioneer no-load funds, if not the first. No-load funds piqued my interest; besides helping a client with their investment and financial planning needs, it also meant that they would only have to pay a very nominal fee every quarter for management, much lower than competing firms. With lower overhead costs, unlike the majority of brokerage firms, Vanguard could undercut its competitor's fee structures by significant percentages. It seemed to me, the purest form of helping clients, and that resonated with me. Though I always strived to discount fees for clients and keep their best interests in the forefront of whatever I recommended, there was no way to get around higher fees altogether. Vanguard management realized they could make a handsome profit and still provide their clients the best value proposition in the industry.

After quite some time enjoying our conversation with my former manager and his wife, I realized it was getting late. Upon leaving, Dave approached me from a business standpoint, wanting to know if I was interested in pursuing Vanguard and the new department. He mentioned if I gave him a resume he would make sure it arrived in the proper hands. I thanked him, took his number, and said I would think about it and call him in a week or so.

As I wheeled out of the restaurant toward my van, my mind was spinning with all that had happened that night. We arrived home, and as I went to sleep, I worked to free my mind of all the events of that evening. I had been employed without foreseeable monthly income, being in a commission-oriented structure, for years. No paid holidays, vacation days or sick days in my career so far, let alone short or long-term disability. I had never really concerned myself with those typical corporate offerings before, as naïve as that may sound. I was making a good income from generating ideas for my clients and had thankfully stayed healthy.

The next morning, I realized I should at least explore this new department Vanguard had formed. If nothing else, I could come away with an understanding of what they did, and begin to consider what would be the impact on my clients, and how they may feel if I left where

I was. I called Dave the following Friday. I mentioned that I would send him an updated resume the next Monday. As promised a week earlier, he let me know that he would forward it to the department I was interested in exploring. I thanked him and went back to work that Monday after dropping my resume in the mail.

The following week someone from Vanguard Human Resources called—they were interested in talking to me. They had received my resume and wanted to interview me for Asset Management Services as an investment manager. I had enjoyed my Vanguard experience years earlier working part-time, limited though it was at the time in the scope and depth I wanted to pursue. I was now interested in learning what this new department at Vanguard offered investment managers as far as a career path, how much flexibility their financial advisors had managing client accounts and more detail around job benefits and security. I didn't have any strong idea what they offered. No one I ever knew worked in the department at Vanguard I was exploring. Also, I didn't have time to discuss with my former manager all the employee benefits when I ran into him a couple of weeks ago at he restaurant.

Before the interview, I did learn that I would be meeting individually with four separate managers in the department for about an hour each, one after the other. First, with the head of the department, then two direct reports to him, finishing the last interview with a staff manager who had about six financial advisors who reported directly to them. They told me the interviews would run concurrently, starting at noon and would last about five hours, with ten-minute breaks in between.

On the day of the interview, my assistant and I drove through Vanguard's large campus. I was impressed; it looked more like a big college campus, complete with a bell tower, immaculately kept grounds and several outdoor areas that had been well laid out. Years earlier, the Investor Information Department where I had worked part-time was at a different location, consisting of separate buildings, not on an elaborate campus like this. I wheeled into the building and went to the floor where the department was located. I noticed it was much quieter than the firms I was previously with, not even close to appearing as "busy" as Merrill. No one was running around and submitting buy or sell tickets, or standing with a headset on, talking and gesturing emphatically in space, touting the merits of a particular investment. The department head warmly greeted my assistant and me. She shook his hand, and he motioned for me to follow him into a large conference room.

As before, I never had an assistant accompany me into an interview, and she patiently waited in a beautiful sitting area. I began to discuss my background with the department head and what types of financial planning I specialized in. I began to ask questions regarding what they offered clients, on to what kind of person usually signed up for their advisory services. After his comments, I realized clearly that this service was much deeper in breadth and scope regarding financial planning than what my previous firm offered. Everything from estate plan reviews involving trusts, to tax considerations, Roth conversion analysis, educational planning for children's college expenses, to robust analysis on the placement of client assets for best tax efficiency and performance. So many more opportunities for customers than I had ever known. Equally impressive, they also generated individual reports for those joining the service, clarifying in sharp detail what was recommended. Even quarterly performance reports and annual follow-up reports, just in case there were any recommended changes to their asset mix or their income and expenses had changed from the prior year. I began to see the benefits to the client and myself.

After five hours and four interviews with senior staff and one staff manager, I was hopeful that they liked what I brought in experience and knowledge. I knew if I left my current position, there would be many more demands educationally, mostly around greater in-depth financial planning and strategies for the client. My compensation structure with Vanguard would be salary-based, with modest bonus potential, and less uncertain than in my previous commission-based arrangements. I left around five that evening, ready to get outdoors.

All four consecutive and intensive interviews were different; each interviewer was interested in targeting specific areas. With these four interviewers, I had no concrete ideas about how to gauge their thoughts. Let alone, where they may have stood, individually or as a group, on my potential to fit into their philosophy and structure. As we drove out of Vanguard, I wasn't anxious or nervous, and throughout the whole interview process, felt remarkably calm. One detail worth noting; the second in command who also interviewed me had attended Merrill's training as well in Princeton.

He and I enjoyed recounting our time at Merrill, the intense training program and I'm sure it didn't hurt having that connection. He spent four years with Merrill as well, before he left for other opportunities. The interviewers were all sharp and well spoken, but more importantly, they were direct and serious, as was I. They shared that the department was looking to continue to build their financial advisor base slowly, and was not in any hurry to hire, potentially three or four financial advisors a year. Though the department was about two years old, they had grown internally through hiring from other departments within Vanguard. I later learned that some, like me, came in from the outside, some from banks or recruited from other financial firms. A few of the interviewers confided that manageable size within the department had already been reached with thirty or so investment managers.

Upon leaving, I had no idea whether the information shared about advisor capacity was based on clients and assets, the pace of new customers coming in to join, or what criteria they were using to decide. I thought the interviews had gone well from my limited perspective but wasn't sure if I met what they were looking for.

I received a phone call from Vanguard the next day. I had just arrived home from work, and it was from their Human Resources department. They wanted to offer me a position and discuss the salary and benefits. I shared my interest, though mentioned it would depend on the starting salary. I explained I had a nice sized mortgage and required a certain level to meet my spending needs. After some discussion and raising the base salary to an agreeable amount, we were able to come to a verbal agreement. They would mail the necessary paperwork, the booklet on their benefits plan, among other things.

I had asked for a month to contact and explain to clients at the firm where I was employed, my new direction. I expressed my interest in helping them transition to Vanguard if they desired. I put together a letter as well, relaying that I was going to leave the brokerage industry, and would be concentrating more on pure financial planning. All of my clients were familiar with Vanguard, many of them confided they had accounts there already, in addition to the ones they held with me. I also alerted my manager that I was leaving the firm. My clients who stayed with the firm would continue to receive support from the sales staff, and be assigned to other brokers within the office, to help them with their trades. It was a decision that would ensure my clients that stayed behind would be well taken care of when I left.

I was looking forward to this career move. Though it would be challenging and demanding, not unlike the other firms I was previously employed by, I recognized the opportunities for me as well. I would be expanding my knowledge base and delving deeper into financial planning with new clients coming in, much more extensive than in the past. I was ready to learn more, and as a result, grow personally as a money manager. The more stable salary and benefits package would also provide a buffer against unexpected health care setbacks. Their healthcare offerings seemed to be similar to what many large corporations provided. I would also now be receiving paid sick days and holidays, as well as three weeks paid vacation starting out. That was exciting enough, and I would even enjoy additional vacation weeks further into my career, along with contributions to my retirement plan and increases in partnership payouts as well as bonuses. Of course, like any firm, my performance reviews would dictate any salary or merit increases I might receive going forward, let alone keeping my position with the company.

All things considered, the choice of which way to continue with my career path became clear, after I weighed my options. I knew my decision to move on with Vanguard would be much less uncertain going forward than it was in the brokerage world. Plus, I was looking forward to the change of direction the new position at Vanguard would offer.

After fond farewells to my clients and brokers in the office, a week later I went through Vanguard's training program. The introductory meeting was very relaxed; nowhere near the intensity of Merrill's when I started my career. This session was strictly about reaching out to all new hires within their large organization, covering everything from Vanguard's philosophy, to employee benefits and words of welcome. The specific training would come later, within the department I was hired in. I looked forward to the new opportunities I would experience with this industry leader.

Pictured with my dad after arriving home after work.
He was leaving for a black tie affair.

Besides being relatively new, the department where I would be employed was run by very conscientious and dedicated people. Even more noteworthy was their primary focus, which was to offer the clients who enrolled in their unparalleled service, objectivity, value, and comprehensive planning. All the financial advisors were on salary, removing all possible conflicts of interest. The funds used in their asset allocation models also had some of the lowest expense ratios in the industry. You couldn't help but appreciate that they offered one of the purest, inexpensive and most objective value proposition available to clients worldwide.

Due to Vanguard's strong reputation and the trust they had established with their customers over the years, there was no need to solicit or cold call for business in this new advisory service. That meant instead of me spending the time to drum up a new business, the clients who came to this department for financial planning services came of their own volition. When they learned through literature, or on Vanguard's website, that there was now a low-cost, comprehensive advisory service available, many signed up. The department also had a business development group, where all prospects coming in would fill out a comprehensive financial profile plan. Our department, instead of just randomly assigning clients, had us provide any state, client background, or particular financial planning areas that we enjoyed. By adopting this approach, it was easier to develop a front-end rapport with a new client. Equally important, their financial advisor would enjoy these commonalities with the hopes the relationship would flourish and be long-term in nature.

As I had graduated from Texas A&M and had relatives and friends in Texas and Oklahoma, I was fortunate to work with about twenty percent of my client base who were from these states. I also understood the oil business to some degree, from buying oil companies, pipelines, explorers, or refiner's shares through the years for clients when I was with Merrill. I would help position them in this sector when advantageous, and became quite knowledgeable as well in miners, pharmaceuticals, and the healthcare field. I requested to work with clients who had either been employed in these sectors or were still working there in some capacity. About twelve of my clients were in the healthcare field and ranged from neurosurgeons, anesthesiologists, oral surgeons, urology, orthopedics and primary care. They were familiar with cervical injuries, and when probed I would share my disability and enjoyed our discussions concerning healthcare. I even had a few clients who were A&M graduates decades earlier. It was enjoyable catching up with these clients on the news concerning the University, Aggie football, among many other things. Some were still living right in Bryan-College Station where the University is located.

Some clients brought assets for me to manage, in the form of stock shares left to them by a long-passed relative. These clients would share stories of how an astute grandmother or grandfather they knew in their youth had liked a particular company and their business, and decided to buy some shares. In many cases, enjoying splits, spin-offs, mergers, and multiple dividend increases. Others had inherited multiple diversified companies and rode them to great success.

The vast majority of my clients had realized long-term success, through saving, hard work, frugal lifestyles and diversified investing. Trying to plan ahead with the environments they were presented. Many clients didn't inherit much beyond memories and experiences, some good and some sad. Often these investors were in their early sixties to late nineties and had lived through and experienced first-hand the impact of many rough periods. Many as children, were exposed to depression era conditions, world wars, recessions, and huge inflation. They were amazing, personable and fun to work with, as one can imagine.

As the department grew, the number of clients we individually managed increased as well as the assets entrusted for us to invest. After some years had gone by, I was promoted to a Senior Investment Advisor position and helped chair an investment committee later in my career. It was fun and enjoyable, sharing my knowledge and experience with other advisors in the department. The committee was dynamic, discussing everything from asset allocation, to markets in the US and abroad, world events, and many other things that may impact client's portfolios. As a result, the meetings were always fresh and informative. After working in this department for quite a few years managing several hundred million for clients, and enjoying a successful career, I thought about pursuing other things.

First *Things* First
Reaffirming our commitment to excellent client service

From the desk of Bill McNabb

It has been a fabulous first month, in terms of service levels, business results, and cash flow. Thanks for all the great efforts!

Bill

Bill McNabb
Managing Director
Client Relationship Group

The Client Relationship Group's First Things First campaign this January has set a new record, with over 1,800 nominations filled with examples of unmatchable excellence, teamwork, client focus, and GREAT people management. I applaud the work of this year's awardees and the hard work and dedication of all CRG crew members. 2006 is off to a great start, thanks to you. As we conclude our First Things First campaign this month, please accept this gift as a reminder that the principles of First Things First are important throughout the year. Thank you for all you do, every day, to serve Vanguard's clients.

A recognition note from CEO Bill McNabb to the
Vanguard crew for a job well done.

Over the years, I had been asked by several groups to speak publicly, some of the groups, multiple times. Many of my talks centered on my accident, how I overcame obstacles and challenges by setting goals, and my career. I would also share what insights and knowledge I had gained since my accident, so many years earlier. After much thought, I came to a difficult decision. I decided to leave my money management career.

I knew letting my manager know of my decision to leave Vanguard wouldn't be easy. I had met many truly terrific people while there, cultivating strong friendships in the process. I also developed some excellent client relationships, several spanning ten years, and they had become like family to me. Many would share pictures, grandkids graduations, family memories, experiences, travel destinations and speak breathlessly of the journeys they had undertaken.

Many of my clients wanted me to know everything, something I wholeheartedly endorsed as well. This enabled me to make the best and most informed decisions on their behalf and helped immensely in their financial planning. Our conversations ranged from discussing their health and the health of loved ones, their hopes and concerns, on-going family matters, plans in retirement, and how their estate would be distributed when they passed on. I helped them navigate through many challenging issues and sad moments, from the financial impact and subsequent emotional toll due to debilitating mental and physical conditions, along with devastating life-taking disease.

The process of dispersing my client base was almost halfway complete, or about six weeks into the three months I had given Vanguard to properly transition my clients when I experienced a significant health-related setback. I had never been out on sick leave for any length of time while at Vanguard. Over several days, I developed a high fever due to an unchecked urinary tract infection (UTI). The infection was untreatable with standard, oral antibiotics, and I ended up requiring a lengthy hospital stay and recovery time. It would mark the first time I was hospitalized since my car accident years earlier. The infection unfortunately was extreme, eventually affecting my hipbones, requiring surgeries on both sides. I again experienced high fevers for quite some time as a result, and heart arrhythmia, due to the pernicious nature of the strain.

There were no hallucinations or mind tricks this time around, unlike my first lengthy hospital experience from the car accident. I had started meditation years earlier, and unlike my first run as a newly trained conductor experimenting with creative imagery to get me past the greatest challenge of my life, I didn't feel intimidated or fearful this time around, now able to control my environment with greater clarity.

After finally getting out of the hospital five weeks later, I came home with a PICC line in my chest, which is a peripherally inserted central catheter pumping antibiotics throughout my system. I was pretty darn tired and still sick, but recovering. One thing I don't think anyone can easily conquer is feeling rested coming out of a hospital setting! I also had to convalesce at home for a minimum of two months. I was weak and couldn't stay up in my chair for any length of time until my hips healed. In the meantime, the rest of my clients were fortunately reassigned to the financial advisors that were handpicked for them before my setback.

Farewell, and Many Thanks!

Please join me in congratulating Dave Rippy on his decision to move on to the next phase of his life. Dave began his career at Vanguard in 1998.

Dave spent his entire career as a Financial Advisor through the many different permutations of AMS; Personal Advisory Services, Personal Trust Service, Trust & Advisory Services and now Asset Management Services. I have had the pleasure of working with Dave over the last few years and his knowledge and market commentary will be sorely missed.

Dave shared with me some of the things he is excited about moving ahead with which will provide a lot of benefit to those individuals and families that have been impacted by various physical limitations, born with or develop in their lives for example, MS, various cancers, disabilities, etc. He hopes that by sharing his experiences and knowledge, that it could hopefully make their quality of life less difficult and uncertain on which direction to turn to for advice, knowledge and general ideas to help alleviate their burdens.

Some of you may not know; Dave writes on the side and has been working on various educational videos and a book in his spare time which he thinks will help many people in the future with a host of concerns, from equipping vehicles with adaptive equipment, to hiring assistants, setting goals to get a job, home renovations, etc. When they are completed, Dave has assured us that if anyone needs a video, he will do it at a discount, as he has told us that he will miss working with such a fine group of people with such a strong philosophy of doing the "right thing".

Dave's experience and expertise will be missed! I would like to thank Dave for all of his contributions and congratulate him for all he has done for the organization over the years. We wish Dave a lot of success in the future and he is working with all involved to make the client transitions as seamless as possible.

Farewell letter from the department.

Though I was paid handsomely to serve in the capacity as their money manager for many clients at multiple firms, equally enjoyable and rewarding was the opportunity to be a part of my client's lives. Helping to benefit them in whatever small way I could.

Forks in the Road

ALL OF US HAVE ENCOUNTERED forks on our own road through life. Forks that we experience and looking back over our shoulder with hindsight wonder, *"What if I had…?"* All paths we choose, or just find ourselves on, present us with different life experiences and lessons, regardless of how they come into our lives. My car accident found me veering down a different road at a fork, and on a new route that was much harder to navigate than the path I had envisioned for myself only twenty-four hours earlier. Going forward was the only option, as it was impossible to turn around and take the alternate way.

This new road would present much more formidable challenges to overcome. Since I was no longer able-bodied, every step in my life would now require more thought, coordination, and planning than ever before. One obvious road sign that came up suddenly on this unfamiliar stretch was the need to hire assistants. Assistants who could help me to accomplish the goals I would eventually establish and contribute to making my life more independent. Without their assistance, the number of things I could accomplish alone was limited. With support, it seemed to me that many more things would be possible, my dreams more practical and the way forward full of opportunities yet to be discovered.

For those who have just been through a horrific or challenging situation and some time has passed, keep that in mind; the way forward will most likely be easier than what you just went through. I knew that living with paralysis would not be all downhill from here on out, but at least hopefully, flat land or a gently sloping hill to traverse for a while. Providing me some time to get my bearings back and whatever that meant or would lead to.

I would now be living with the aftermath of my accident, not unlike many of you, or your friends or family members. Not easy for anyone who has known suffering. Looking back at your life prior, the hardest part is seeing anything positive on this new highway you find yourself on. Though it is there in plain sight. Through our challenges and tough times, though unwelcome, come greater realizations and knowledge of who we are, as unique human beings, and what we are capable of accomplishing. Perhaps we are now wearing some visible and not so visible badges. Badges that we earned, tests we passed, when early on, we may have thought we never would get through it all.

Sometimes on our road of life, what looked bright and sunny in the distance brings unimaginable storms of darkness into what were moments earlier, blue and promising skies. As we struggle along through these unexpected, turbulent periods, sometimes so powerful, we are blown off what we envisioned as our life's course. Now much farther away from where we just were.

Many of us, with or without help, will struggle back onto our knees, then onto our feet again, barely inching forward as we push back against the harsh and punishing winds of our new reality. The darkness seemingly haunting and mocking us, as we fight through.

Winston Churchill once said, *"If you are going through hell, keep going."* Every one of us, at one time, or another, will encounter hellish times and challenging circumstances. All we can do is work hard and move past the incident as best we can. Walls and barriers are not placed in our path to stop us, simply as lessons and experiences for us to circumnavigate, or scale, as sad and painful as many can be. If all of us didn't have some degree of drive, or the desire to persevere, our oceans, mountains, deserts and plains, may have just remained unexplored and untested. Our species relegated to specific areas, never growing, advancing, let alone *evolving*.

Once we move beyond our challenging times, hopefully to a stretch of clear skies on our road, an easier way. When we eventually find that space and peace again, our journey forward becomes more gentle, joyful and uplifting. Despite our struggles, our sacrificing and pain, we made it. Afterward, we have a greater view and understanding of our strengths and ourselves in the process. However challenging and sad, we can't change the past, only the moment at hand and our future. If we focus on what we have gained and not on what was lost, hard as it is sometimes to see, it will enable us to start moving toward a future we want.

All of us, figuratively speaking, are the captains of our souls, and the sole pioneer taking us towards our eventual destiny or destinies. Sure, we may have a spouse, family, friends, love interests, or parents who are along in some cases, for a good part. Though where we eventually journey is up to us, no one else leads our life and no one else experiences what we do as individuals. What you have eaten, breathed, believed, heard and seen, has only been experienced by you. No one else has processed exactly what you alone experienced. The beaches, buildings, brick roads and battlegrounds you've visited and walked, not one other person has ever made that journey, before and nor will anyone afterward be able to retrace your steps. All you have heard, witnessed and dreamed about has only originated through you. Everything you've experienced is the beginning foundations of what you later create for yourself, leading to further discoveries and experiences.

The author, Hermann Hesse once remarked, *"The goal of life is to find yourself."* Meaning only through discovery and experiences in life, do we learn more about ourselves, and who we are, regardless of the way. If your life takes a turn at a fork that wasn't expected or welcome, encountering a rough patch or hellish experience; scream, yell with anger, and cry, if it helps move you forward. If you can, punch a speed bag, run, walk on the beach or in the woods, read, write, talk it over with friends, professionals—do whatever it takes to let it go.

Then continue where you left off, to whatever degree possible. Pick yourself up and sling over your shoulder again the "life backpack" you're tasked with taking on your journey. Even the new, cumbersome and un-wanted contents you are now carrying along, with what was there before your life took a turn. If some things are burdening you, weighing you down, and you can discard, let them go. Start walking down your road again.

There will be others along the many roads of your life, different forks you can choose, and some paths you just end up on. All will present different outcomes and possibilities along the way. Some routes can branch off and eventually rejoin the road left before, maybe a direction or destination more preferred.

Along the way, some you encounter may want to help you, join you, love you, just talk, share things or become friends with you. Others will try to slow you down, maybe take you down an undesired route, and some will be carrying hurts and pains they can't seem to discard or work through. Others sadly, may be hurtful or scare you.

Each step, every moment along the way, is going to be different, though maybe that is not apparent all the time. Sometimes so subtle, the difference is barely perceptible to us, but that instant, that moment was full of change. The more you capture, retain and experience *good* or *bad* in life, brings not only wonderful or sad memories but more importantly, a greater knowledge of yourself and *who you are as an individual.*

Many of us, like millions across the globe, are shouldering challenges, attempting to meet our struggles head on. Regardless of the route we take or find ourselves on, we continue to grow and learn in the process. No words spoken or on a page can adequately capture the true extent of some human struggles, simply living them, day in and day out. Now etched in the minds and memories of those who endure and carry on, often to their limits, learning more about themselves along the way.

Sadly, many aren't aware of the value of life's lessons, and the strengths and wisdom they have *earned* in carrying heavy burdens. Often, they perceive these challenges and setbacks as the hard hand they've been dealt, bad luck, horrible and somehow they deserve it, perhaps seeing themselves as unworthy or unfit for good things. Nothing could be farther from the truth; your life experiences, whether good or bad, can provide valuable insights, lessons and the needed "ingredients" to move you forward.

From the millions who are mentally or physically affected by war to those suffering from disease, the loss of a loved one, a painful divorce, incarceration, abuse, exploitation, to those born with disabilities or acquired later in life, like me: many choose to continue on. Their stories, all different from mine, are not any less special, and in many cases, are much more challenging.

Our mindset and perceptions, during and after tumultuous events, will often dictate whether they will remain insurmountable or lead to greater realizations, enabling us to free ourselves and move forward.

The road of our life will always present us with forks, detours, speed bumps, dangerous curves, straightaways, dizzying drops as well as uplifting and beautiful vistas. There will be many on our path at times, and occasionally, a stretch or journey that we undertake alone. There will be times that seem to go on forever and others that end in a blink of the eye. There will be moments we stop, breathe and take in what we encounter, perhaps staying in one spot for a while. Once in awhile, we'll just want to see what's around the next bend. On occasion, we'll stray off our road, maybe noticing something that distracts and draws our attention.

Often, we won't remember what we just passed, perhaps encountered, too busy in our haste to notice. Losing those opportunities, those moments, that are now gone forever. Moments that we failed to appreciate, memories we didn't fully capture, and further down our road, looking back over our shoulder, wishing we had. Thinking, 'they were right there for me to grasp at the time, *why didn't I?*'

As the years and miles add up on our journey, we will find ourselves time and time again, turning around, looking back over those roads we had already traveled in our minds. Thinking, with the beauty of hindsight on our side, if along the way, I had just breathed more, thought more, and captured more of those moments I let go.

Reflecting, once again, *"what if I had...?"*

Conclusion

*"By three methods we may learn wisdom: First, by reflection,
which is noblest; Second, by imitation, which is easiest;
and third by experience, which is the bitterest."*

—Confucius

*"The road of Knowledge has many pitfalls; as you encounter, stumble
and right yourself again, hopefully, it will lead to Wisdom."*

UP TO THE ACCIDENT, MY life was mostly clear sailing. Afterward, from getting to the emergency room in time, to my career and subsequent life; I have been blessed, and in many ways, my life has been miraculous. Some will believe that it was from setting goals that I would eventually accomplish, an amazing family and support system, perhaps luck, plain hard work or with divine help. I firmly believe it was due to all of these factors.

I also believe I will regain my full body function someday. The miracle of walking again is planted firmly in my heart, knowing that regardless of the timeframe, it will take place. Upbeat thoughts pass through my mind as I contemplate that possibility, and the sheer magnitude of what that means not only to me but those in my family, my friends, and hopefully others.

Many might consider my thoughts on walking again a delusion, a well-crafted fantasy, or possibly just a way to escape the life I've lived for so many days and nights. However, I believe otherwise, knowing that through the power of our mind, prayer and GOD, miracles do exist.

Looking back over my life until now and what I've learned, experienced, and gathered through the years, I've already witnessed many miracles. The miracles that occur every day often go unnoticed, whether in nature, the cosmos or to humanity itself. I believe more miracles will come, not only in my life, but in the lives of many others as we all go forward on our individual journeys.

Also, I hope my journey provides some insight, ideas, and awareness, that all of us can attain what we seek, rise to heights we never realized and *"carry"* the power of the divine within. Believing in ourselves, our uniqueness, and forming a vision can take us a long way.

It really is up to us.

> *"And so I tell you, keep on asking, and you will receive what you ask for. Keep on seeking, and you will find. Keep on knocking, and the door will be opened to you. For everyone who asks, receives. Everyone who seeks, finds. And to everyone who knocks, the door will be opened." (Luke 11:9-10)*

—JESUS

> *"Acquire knowledge. It enables its possessor to distinguish right from wrong, it lights the way to Heaven, it is our friend in the desert, our society in solitude, our companion when friendless, it guides us to happiness, it sustains us in misery, it is an ornament among friends and an armor against enemies."*

—PROPHET MOHAMMED

"It does not matter how slowly you go as long as you do not stop."

—CONFUCIUS

"The weak can never forgive. Forgiveness is an attribute of the strong."

—GHANDI

"There is no need for temples, no need for complicated philosophies. My brain and my heart are my temples; my philosophy is kindness."

—DALAI LAMA

"The most authentic thing about us is our capacity to create, to overcome, to endure, to transform, to love and to be greater than our suffering."

—BEN OKRI

"We ourselves feel that what we are doing is just a drop in the ocean. But the ocean would be less because of that missing drop."

—MOTHER TERESA

"The person who says it cannot be done should not interrupt the person who is doing it."

—CHINESE PROVERB

"Your present circumstances don't determine where you can go; they merely determine where you start."

—NIDO QUBEIN

*"You have to learn the rules of the game. And then
you have to play better than anyone else."*

—ALBERT EINSTEIN

*"There is no person so severely punished, as those who
subject themselves to the whip of their own remorse."*

—SENECA

*"When we quit thinking primarily about ourselves,
and our own self-preservation, we undergo a truly
heroic transformation of consciousness."*

—JOSEPH CAMPBELL

*"Let me embrace thee, sour adversity, for wise
men say it is the wisest course."*

—WILLIAM SHAKESPEARE

*"It isn't what we don't know that gives us trouble,
it's what we know that just ain't so."*

—WILL ROGERS

*"Life is thickly sown with thorns, and I know no other remedy
than to pass quickly through them. The longer we dwell on
our misfortunes, the greater is their power to harm us."*

—VOLTAIRE

"Do not worry about tomorrow, for tomorrow will worry about itself. Each day has enough trouble of its own."

–(MATTHEW 6:34)
—JESUS

"Strength does not come from physical capacity. It comes from an indomitable will."

—GHANDI

"Men's best successes come after their disappointments."

—HENRY WARD BEECHER

"The gem cannot be polished without friction nor man without trials."

—CONFUCIUS

"We can easily forgive a child who is afraid of the dark; the real tragedy of life is when men are afraid of the light."

—PLATO

"We must embrace pain and burn it as fuel for our journey."

—KENJI MIYAZAWA

*"Do not say that if people do good to us, we will do good
to them and if people oppress us, we will oppress them but
determine that if people do you good, you will do good to them
and if they oppress you, you will not oppress them."*

—PROPHET MOHAMMED

*"That deep emotional conviction of the presence of
a superior reasoning power, which is revealed in the
incomprehensible universe, forms my idea of God."*

—ALBERT EINSTEIN

"Luck is where opportunity meets preparation."

—SENECA

Prayer

Oh, Great Spirit
Whose voice I hear in the winds,
And whose breath gives life to all the world,
hear me, I am small and weak,
I need your strength and wisdom.
Let me walk in beauty and make my eyes ever behold
the red and purple sunset.
Make my hands respect the things you have
made and my ears sharp to hear your voice.
Make me wise so that I may understand the things
you have taught my people.
Let me learn the lessons you have
hidden in every leaf and rock.
I seek strength, not to be greater than my brother,
but to fight my greatest enemy - myself.
Make me always ready to come to you
with clean hands and straight eyes.
So when life fades, as the fading sunset,
my Spirit may come to you without shame.

Native American Prayer

Acknowledgements

In concluding this part of my journey, I'd like to acknowledge those to whom I owe a great deal of gratitude. First and foremost, to my mother and father – your support has been unwavering, and your love has made my journey easier than it would have been otherwise. A special thanks to my sister Melinda, your insights concerning the book were "spot on" and you have definitely made my life easier and smoother. To my three brothers, thank you for always being present in so many ways. I would be remiss to not thank my sibling-in-laws Kolleen, Peggy and Ralph for all you have done for me. To my nephews and niece, Matthew, Taylor, Sam, Kellie and Tyler, you are all amazing!

To all the assistants who have been in my life since those early days of living with paralysis till now, I am forever grateful for your help. This book and my subsequent journey would not have been possible without your support, dedication and love. To my editor and assistant Amy Patt; thank you for all of your efforts and creative insights. You have made this a better book than it otherwise might have been. A big thanks to my niece Kellie for reviewing and to Stephanie, Donna, Josey, for your input as well. A special thank you to my friend, Max, for taking this book to the next level. To Elisabeth, who has made my days brighter, my heart lighter, and brings joy and fullness to my world. And to you, my dear reader, thank you for taking the time to read my story.

Best regards,
David

About the Author

DAVID RIPPY ATTENDED VILLANOVA UNIVERSITY before graduating from Texas A&M University with a Bachelor of Science degree in Economics. At age twenty-five, he was just beginning a career at a Fortune 50 company when a car accident left him paralyzed from the shoulders down.

Despite this life-altering injury, he formulated a vision for his life. He became determined to fulfill his ambition to become a money manager—and he did. David went on to have a long and successful career. He worked at Merrill Lynch and the Vanguard Group for years and acquired various certifications and licenses in the process.

Today, he's left the finance field to write, speak, inspire and help others by sharing the story of his own perseverance and triumph. He still believes that there are more miracles to come in his life, and works toward new goals and aspirations every day.

Made in the USA
Middletown, DE
19 March 2017